The Logic Manual

VOLKER HALBACH

OXFORD

UNIVERSITY PRESS

OXFORD

UNIVERSITY PRESS

Great Clarendon Street, Oxford OX2 6DP
United Kingdom

Oxford University Press is a department of the University of Oxford.
It furthers the University's objective of excellence in research, scholarship,
and education by publishing worldwide.
Oxford is a registered trade mark of Oxford University Press in the UK
and in certain other countries

Reprinted 2015 with corrections

British Library Cataloguing in Publication Data
Data available

Library of Congress Cataloging in Publication Data
Data available

ISBN 978-0-19-958784-1

THE LOGIC MANUAL

Contents

About the Logic Manual

The Logic Manual is a concise introduction to logic up to and including the semantics and a proof system for predicate logic with identity.

My main objective in writing the Manual was to prepare the reader for understanding important philosophical texts, mainly in the analytic tradition.

The semantics of predicate logic and the definition of satisfaction figure prominently in modern philosophy of language and not only there. I have therefore included a fairly detailed account of truth in a structure, as an acquaintance with the notions of a variable assignment, a model, and satisfaction is presupposed in many texts.

For similar reasons, I have chosen a system of Natural Deduction as the proof system. Since its terminology is used in the philosophy of language and elsewhere, it is more useful for most philosophy students to know what introduction and elimination rules are and what it means to discharge an assumption than to be acquainted with a tableau system, even though the latter lends itself more easily to a completeness proof.

Even when new concepts are introduced by means of examples or informal explanations, I have always strived to include general abstract definitions, not so much for the sake of logical pedantry but rather to acquaint the reader with a general abstract way of thinking about language, logic, and semantics. The ability to reason about the relevant concepts in precise and general terms is presumably even more important for a philosopher than some virtuosity in calculating truth tables or proving theorems in some formal system.

I have set the core definitions, explanations, and results *in italics like this*. This might be useful for revision or for finding important passages more quickly. The symbol □ marks the end of a proof.

LEARNING FROM THE MANUAL

The Manual should be used in conjunction with the additional documents and, in particular, with the Exercises Booklet found on the following web page:

http://logicmanual.philosophy.ox.ac.uk

Occasionally I refer to particular exercises in the Exercises Booklet, which can be found on the web page above.

TEACHING FROM THE MANUAL

The above mentioned web page also contains information on how to obtain an instructor's copy of the Exercises Booklet, which includes solutions.

If the material in the Logic Manual is to be covered in two teaching units, then its content can be naturally divided as follows: Chapters 1–3 constitute an introduction to propositional logic, to which Section 6.1 (Natural Deduction for propositional logic) can be added. The remaining Chapters 4–8 yield an introduction to predicate logic with identity, from which the final chapter on identity can be omitted if time is scarce.

In what follows I will briefly comment on some of the individual chapters and give some hints about potential problems for teaching.

In my brief sketch of elementary set-theoretic terminology in Sections 1.1–1.4, I do not discuss the distinction between sets and proper classes. For the sake of set-theoretic hygiene, however, the instructor should avoid calling proper classes sets. In particular, in the semantics of predicate logic, proper classes should not be used as domains of structures and therefore will never contain all sets or all ordered pairs.

In Section 1.5 I introduce the notion of a logically valid argument. I try to keep my characterization of logical validity fairly neutral between an interpretational and representational conception; but I do rule out a definition of logical validity in terms of possible worlds or possible situations as this risks conflating logical truth with other kinds of necessity.

In propositional as well as in predicate logic, I distinguish sharply between translations from formal languages into English on the one hand and formal models or structures on the other. Generally, I aim to avoid the impression that the semantics is parasitic on English: the semantics of the formal languages is presented as something independent from English. Although the semantics is described in English, it could be equally well presented in some other language. In general, students should be urged not to confuse structures with dictionaries that map the non-logical vocabulary of the formal language to English expressions.

Therefore a counterexample should always be understood as a formal structure, rather than a dictionary for the non-logical symbols in the sentences of the argument. I think this is a conceptually important point: a translation from a formal language into English remains at a purely linguistic level, while a formal structure assigns (possibly) non-linguistic objects to the non-logical symbols of the formal language, irrespective of whether the formal structure can be described in English. In fact, as there are uncountably many structures, most structures cannot be specified in any given countable language. Of course, when a specific structure is described, this has to be carried out in a language. But in doing so one should specify suitable objects to assign to the non-logical symbols rather than simply translating them into English. Hence the domain should be specified as a set, predicate letters should be interpreted as set-theoretic relations not as translations of English predicate expressions, and so on.

Moreover, if formal structures are introduced as mere translations from the formal language into English, a main point of formalization is undermined: In order to establish that an English argument is not valid it seems an odd procedure to translate it into a formal language only to translate it immediately back into English to show that the formal argument is also the translation of an argument that is not valid.

In Chapter 6 I introduce a system of Natural Deduction; the chapter covers propositional and predicate logic in two separate sections. It is possible to teach Natural Deduction for propositional logic much earlier, for instance, after Chapter 3. Also if sufficient time is available, it might be sensible to split the chapter and to spend twice as much time on it than on the other chapters.

There are three reasons for introducing Natural Deduction in a single chapter: First, providing lots of examples of proofs is not a very efficient way of teaching Natural Deduction. Students will have to try to carry out proofs for themselves and then their attempts should be discussed individually. Second, I wanted to keep the chapter short to make it easier to find quickly the basic definitions; additional examples of proofs can be found on the web site. Third, I do not think that too much emphasis need be put on formal proofs. As mentioned above, it is important that students become familiar with such concepts as rules of inference, introduction and elimination rules, and so on. They should understand that logical consequence in first-order predicate logic can be captured by a few rules governing the use of the connectives and quantifiers. But if time is scarce, not too much time need be spent on proving complicated theorems in the formal system.

ACKNOWLEDGEMENTS

I am indebted to colleagues, friends, and students for discussions and comments on previous versions of the text. In particular, I would like to thank Varol Akman, Brian Ball, Stephen Blamey, Courtney Cox, Paolo Crivelli, Geoffrey Ferrari, Raphael Hogarth, Eleanor Holmes, Lindsay Judson, Charles MacRae, Ofra Magidor, David McCarty, Peter Millican, Julian Moehlen, Carlo Nicolai, Alexander Paseau, Annamaria Schiaparelli, Sebastian Sequoiah-Grayson, James Studd, Mark Thakkar, Gabriel Uzquiano, Edward Watson, Lee Walters and David Wiggins. I am especially grateful to Christopher von Bülow and Jane Friedman for proofreading.

Introduction

Philosophers think and reason. If they do so properly, they reason correctly and produce valid arguments. Philosophers also tend to reflect on what they are doing. So it is not surprising that philosophers began to develop theories about sound reasoning and the validity of arguments, that is, they began to do logic.

Using the logicians' terminology one can talk about and criticize arguments and theories. When one says that a hidden premiss has been made explicit, or that an argument should be rejected as a scope fallacy, or that a claim is a logical contradiction or a tautology, or that an argument is valid but its conclusion false, one is using terminology from logic. Acquaintance with this terminology is a prerequisite for reading philosophical texts and for engaging in professional philosophical discussions. Logical methods can also help one to find gaps in arguments and to refute the validity of faulty arguments in philosophy and other disciplines.

The application of logic to individual arguments, however, is not the main interest of logicians and it does not explain why logicians devised the very abstract and sophisticated machinery of modern logic. Philosophers often use the tools of logic for more than simply refuting individual arguments, or similar.

Logic opened the path to much more profound, fascinating, and general results. In discussing a single argument logic may be dispensable, but when, for instance, one tries to establish claims about all possible arguments, logic comes into its own.

To establish very general claims about possible proofs and arguments in English, or about the meaning of sentences and phrases of English, is a difficult task. If one tries to make general statements about natural languages like English, one is confronted with their bewildering complexity. Natural languages possess an enormous variety of stylistic variants, exemplify perplexing and captivating ambiguities, and permit subtle allusions and intimations. Since antiquity logicians have tried to get a grip on language and reasoning by regimenting natural languages, cutting down on the number of stylistic variants, and removing ambiguities. These efforts finally led to the development of purely formal symbolic languages that are supposed to capture the features essential to reasoning in natural languages whilst dispensing with their baffling intricacies.

Many formal languages may be viewed as English stripped from all stylistic adornment and ambiguity to the bare bones required for reasoning. Of course, they are not as flexible, concise, subtle, potentially elegant or rich as natural languages, but they have not been devised to be used in the same way as natural languages. Formal languages have been devised to reason *about*, not so much to reason *in*.

Natural languages are readily put to use by competent speakers but are not easily tractable as objects of research. Symbolic languages, in contrast, are typically awkward to use but because of their relative simplicity it is much easier to reflect upon and draw general conclusions about them. Once languages have been simplified and regimented, one can scrutinize aspects of them that were previously quite intractable. I will give three examples of where formal languages and the methods of logic have been used to obtain insights that would otherwise have been hard to achieve.

First example. In order to show that a conclusion follows from a certain theory, one usually tries to give an argument for the conclusion from the theory's assumptions. Some sort of regimentation may be useful, but regimentation comes into its own when one wishes to show that a given conclusion does not follow from the theory. It will hardly be possible to browse through all potential arguments and check whether they succeed in demonstrating that the conclusion follows from the theory's assumptions. Logicians have devised many ingenious methods for showing that certain sentences do not follow from certain assumptions.

One important case is when neither the sentence nor its negation are consequences of the theory, that is, when the sentence is 'independent' from the theory. A physicist, or mathematician, for instance, may first try to prove a hunch from certain assumptions. If he then gets stuck and starts to doubt his first hunch, he may attempt to refute it by proving its negation. If the sentence is independent from the theory, neither strategy can be successful. In fact some problems in mathematics have turned out to be of this kind and logicians were able to show that certain conjectures were not decidable on the basis of the accepted axioms.

Proofs of logical consistency are another case where one would like to show that a certain sentence does not follow from a theory. A theory is called inconsistent if a contradiction follows from the theory, that is, if a sentence and its negation can be derived from the theory. An inconsistent theory cannot be true. So it is important to know that a theory one is interested in is at least consistent, that is, free from contradiction. Again the tools of logic can be used to establish the consistency of a theory.

Second example. Philosophers have tried to provide semantics for language. They have developed theories about the meanings of sentences and certain words. This may sound like a problem for linguists, but it is at the core of metaphysics. For some philosophers have claimed that abstract or universal objects like properties are required as meanings; while others – known as nominalists – have denied the need for such objects.

One can first try the semantic theories on the highly regimented languages of logic: any semantical theory that fails for these simple languages will also fail for the more complex natural languages.

Semantics usually also yields a theory of truth. Logicians have developed precise formal semantics for formal languages including precise theories of truth. Some philosophers think that these theories yield a solution to the age-old problem of what truth is.

Here logic is no longer used as a tool for thinking about theories concerning other subjects, but in the theory of truth semantics and therefore logic itself becomes the subject of philosophical theorizing.

Third example. So far it may seem that logicians have done every-thing they can to simplify and perhaps trivialize language. But logic has helped to bring out language's ineliminable complexities. Logicians have obtained some disquieting results about the limitations of lan-guage and theorizing.

For instance, philosophers once dreamt of a method for deciding whether a given claim follows from a given theory. Such a method could have practical applications. Whether the theory was medical or meteo-rological, one could determine whether a given claim follows from the theory. If the method were efficient, it could be implemented as a com-puter programme. Mathematicians, for instance, would not have to use all their ingenuity to devise proofs, they could simply use the method, or run the programme, to determine whether their conjectures follow from their axioms. It has been proved that, even without any restric-tions on computing time, hard disk space, processor speed, and the like, there is no such method for formal languages; and if there is no such method for such regimented languages, the hopes that there is one for natural languages are dim.

There are still more puzzling results about impossibilities. As men-tioned above, one would like to prove that one's overall theory is con-sistent. It would be disastrous if one found out after a long time that the theory is pointless because it is contradictory and therefore every-thing follows from it. According to one of the most disquieting results in logic, such a consistency proof is impossible: under fairly general assumptions one cannot prove the consistency of a theory within that very same theory. That means that even disciplines that appear to be founded on solid rock may – for all we know – be founded on sand. Not only does one not have a proof that one's theory is consistent, one even knows that there can be no such proof (if the theory is consistent).

This is the other, darker side of logic. The rudiments of logic, to which the Manual is devoted, are fortunately more on the light side.

1 Sets, Relations, and Arguments

1.1 SETS

Set theory is employed in many disciplines. As such, some acquaintance with the most basic notions of set theory will be useful not only in logic, but also in other areas that rely on formal methods. Set theory is a vast area of mathematical research and of significant philosophical interest. For the purposes of this book, the reader only needs to know a fragment of the fundamentals of set theory.[1]

A set is a collection of objects. These objects may be concrete objects such as persons and planets or non-concrete objects such as numbers or other sets. *The objects in the collection are elements of that set.*

Sets are identical if and only if they have the same elements. Therefore, the set of all animals with kidneys and the set of all animals with a heart are identical, because exactly those animals that have kidneys also have a heart and vice versa.[2] In contrast, the property of having a heart is usually distinguished from the property of having kidneys, although both properties apply to the same objects.

That a is an element of the set S can be expressed symbolically by writing 'a ∈ S'. If a is an element of S, one also says that a is in S or that S contains a.

---

1 There are various mathematical introductions to set theory such as Devlin (1993), Moschovakis (1994), or the more elementary Halmos (1960). In contrast to rigorous expositions of set theory, I will not proceed axiomatically here.

2 I have added this footnote because there are regularly protests with respect to this example, which is due to Quine (1951). For this example only complete and healthy animals are being considered. Even with this restriction the example is not uncontroversial for certain species.

There is exactly one set that contains no elements, namely, the empty set ∅. Obviously, there is only one empty set, because all sets containing no elements contain the same elements, namely none.

There are various ways to denote sets.

One can write down names of the elements, or other designations of the elements, and enclose this list in curly brackets.

The set {London, Munich}, for instance, has exactly two cities as its elements. The set {Munich, London} has the same elements. Therefore, the sets are identical, that is:

$$\{\text{London, Munich}\} = \{\text{Munich, London}\}$$

Thus, if a set is specified by including names for the elements in curly brackets, the order of the names between the brackets does not matter.

The set {the capital of England, Munich} is again the same set because 'the capital of England' is just another way of designating London. {London, Munich, the capital of England} is still the same set: adding another name for London, namely, 'the capital of England', does not add a further element to {London, Munich}.

This method of designating sets has its limitations: sometimes one lacks names for the elements. The method will also fail for sets with infinitely many or even just impractically many elements.

Above I have designated a set by the phrase 'the set of all animals with a heart'. One can also use the following semi-formal expression to designate this set:

$$\{ x : x \text{ is an animal with a heart} \}$$

This is read as 'the set of all animals with a heart'. Similarly, $\{ x : x$ is a natural number bigger than 3 $\}$ is the set of natural numbers bigger than 3, and $\{ x : x$ is blue all over or x is red all over $\}$ is the set of all objects that are blue all over and all objects that are red all over.[3]

---

3 The assumption that any description of this kind actually describes a set is problematic. The so-called Russell paradox imposes some limitations on what sets one can postulate. See Exercise 7.4.

1.2 BINARY RELATIONS

The expression 'is a tiger' applies to some objects, but not to others. There is a set of all objects to which it applies, namely the set $\{\,x\,:\,x$ is a tiger $\}$ containing all tigers and no other objects. The expression 'is a bigger city than', in contrast, does not apply to single objects; rather it relates two objects. It applies to London and Munich (in this order), for instance, because London is a bigger city than Munich. One can also say that the expression 'is a bigger city than' applies to pairs of objects. The set of all pairs to which the expression 'is a bigger city than' applies is called 'the binary relation of *being a bigger city than*' or simply 'the relation of *being a bigger city than*'.[4] This relation contains all pairs with objects d and e such that d is a bigger city than e.[5]

These pairs cannot be understood simply as the sets $\{d, e\}$, such that d is a bigger city than e, because elements of a set are not ordered by the set: as pointed out above, the set $\{$London, Munich$\}$ is the same set as $\{$Munich, London$\}$. So a set with two elements does not have a first or second element. Since London is bigger than Munich, but not vice versa, only the pair with London as first component and Munich as second component should be in the relation of *being a bigger city than*, but not the pair with Munich as first component and London as second component.

Therefore, so-called ordered pairs are used in set theory. They are different from sets with two elements. Ordered pairs, in contrast to sets with two elements, have a first and a second component (and no fur-

---

4 By the qualification 'binary' one distinguishes relations applying to pairs from relations applying to triples and strings of more objects. I will return to non-binary relations in Section 1.4.

5 Often philosophers do not identify relations with sets of pairs. On their terminology relations need to be distinguished from sets of ordered pairs in the same way properties need to be distinguished from sets (see footnote 2). In set theory, however, it is common to refer to sets of ordered pairs as binary relations and I shall follow this usage here.

ther components). The ordered pair ⟨London, Munich⟩ has London as its first component and Munich as its second. ⟨Munich, London⟩ is a different ordered pair, because the two ordered pairs differ in both their first and second components.[6] More formally, an ordered pair ⟨d, e⟩ is identical with ⟨f, g⟩ if and only if $d = f$ and $e = g$. The ordered pair ⟨the largest city in Bavaria, the largest city in the UK⟩ is the same ordered pair as ⟨Munich, London⟩, because they coincide in their first and in their second component. An ordered pair can have the same object as first and second component: ⟨London, London⟩, for instance, has London as its first and second component. ⟨Munich, London⟩ and ⟨London, London⟩ are two different ordered pairs, because they differ in their first components. For the sake of brevity, I will often drop the qualification 'ordered' from 'ordered pair'.

DEFINITION 1.1. *A set is a binary relation if and only if it contains only ordered pairs.*

According to the definition, a set is a binary relation if it does not contain anything that is not an ordered pair. Since the empty set ∅ does not contain anything, it does not contain anything that is not an ordered pair. Therefore, the empty set is a binary relation.

In the following I shall occasionally drop the qualification 'binary' and write 'relation' for 'binary relation', when it is clear that I am dealing with binary relations.

The binary relation of being a bigger city than, that is, the relation that is satisfied by objects d and e if and only if d is a bigger city than e is the following set:

$$\{⟨London, Munich⟩, ⟨ London, Oxford⟩, ⟨Munich, Oxford⟩,$$
$$⟨Paris, Munich⟩, \dots \}$$

In the following definition I will classify binary relations. Later, I

---

6 Using a nice trick, one can dispense with ordered pairs by defining the ordered pair ⟨d, e⟩ as $\{\{d\}, \{d, e\}\}$. The trick will not be used here.

shall illustrate the definitions by examples. Here, and in the following, I shall use 'iff' as an abbreviation for 'if and only if'.

DEFINITION 1.2. *A binary relation R is*

(i) *reflexive on a set S iff for all elements d of S the pair $\langle d, d \rangle$ is an element of R;*

(ii) *symmetric on a set S iff for all elements d, e of S: if $\langle d, e \rangle \in R$ then $\langle e, d \rangle \in R$;*

(iii) *asymmetric on a set S iff for no elements d, e of S: $\langle d, e \rangle \in R$ and $\langle e, d \rangle \in R$;*

(iv) *antisymmetric on a set S iff for no two distinct (that is, different) elements d, e of S: $\langle d, e \rangle \in R$ and $\langle e, d \rangle \in R$;*

(v) *transitive on a set S iff for all elements d, e, f of S: if $\langle d, e \rangle \in R$ and $\langle e, f \rangle \in R$, then also $\langle d, f \rangle \in R$.*

So, for instance, a binary relation is symmetric on S if and only if, considering only ordered pairs with components in S, if a pair is in the relation also the pair with its components reversed is in the relation.

Often the relativization to a set is not needed. A binary relation is symmetric (without relativization, or simpliciter) if and only if it is symmetric on all sets.

DEFINITION 1.3. *A binary relation R is*

(i) *symmetric iff it is symmetric on all sets;*

(ii) *asymmetric iff it is asymmetric on all sets;*

(iii) *antisymmetric iff it is antisymmetric on all sets;*

(iv) *transitive iff it is transitive on all sets.*

So, for instance, a binary relation is symmetric if and only if for any ordered pair in the relation the pair with the components reversed is also in the relation.

Therefore a binary relation R is

(i) symmetric iff for all d, e: if $\langle d, e \rangle \in R$ then $\langle e, d \rangle \in R$;

(ii) asymmetric iff for no d, e: $\langle d, e \rangle \in R$ and $\langle e, d \rangle \in R$;

(iii) antisymmetric iff for no two distinct d, e: $\langle d, e \rangle \in R$ and $\langle e, d \rangle \in R$;

(iv) transitive iff for all d, e, f: if $\langle d, e \rangle \in R$ and $\langle e, f \rangle \in R$, then also
$\langle d, f \rangle \in R$.

As long as they are not too complicated, relations and their properties – such as reflexivity and symmetry – can be visualized by diagrams.
For every component of an ordered pair in the relation, one writes exactly one name (or other designation) in the diagram. The ordered pairs
in the relation are then represented by arrows. For instance, the relation

$$\{\langle \text{France, Italy}\rangle, \langle \text{Italy, Austria}\rangle, \langle \text{France, France}\rangle,$$
$$\langle \text{Italy, Italy}\rangle, \langle \text{Austria, Austria}\rangle\}$$

has the following diagram:

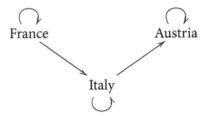

The arrow from 'France' to 'Italy' corresponds to the pair ⟨France,
Italy⟩, and the arrow from 'Italy' to 'Austria' corresponds to the pair
⟨Italy, Austria⟩. The three loops in the diagram correspond to the three
pairs ⟨France, France⟩, ⟨Italy, Italy⟩, ⟨Austria, Austria⟩.

Since 'France', 'Italy', and 'Austria' all have such a loop attached to
them, the relation is reflexive on the set {France, Italy, Austria}. The
relation is not reflexive on larger sets. For instance, it is not reflexive on
the set {France, Italy, Austria, Spain}, because the pair ⟨Spain, Spain⟩
is not in the relation.

The relation is not transitive. For transitivity it is required that if
there is an arrow from a point d to a point e and one from e to f in the
diagram, then there must be a 'short cut', that is, a (direct) arrow from d
to f. In the diagram above there is an arrow from 'France' to 'Italy' and
an arrow from 'Italy' to 'Austria', but there is no arrow from 'France'

to 'Austria'. Hence the relation is not transitive. If the additional pair ⟨France, Austria⟩ were added to the relation, then a transitive relation would be obtained.

The relation is transitive on the set {France, Italy} because if Austria is dropped from the diagram there is no missing short cut. It is also transitive on {Italy, Austria} and {France, Austria}, but it is not transitive on any set containing all three countries France, Italy, and Austria.

If a relation is symmetric, then there are no 'one-way' arrows. That is, if there is an arrow from d to e, then there must be an arrow back to d from e. The relation above is not symmetric. For instance, the pair ⟨France, Italy⟩ is in the relation, but not the pair ⟨Italy, France⟩. That is, in the diagram there is an arrow from 'France' to 'Italy' but no arrow back from 'Italy' to 'France'.

The relation is also not asymmetric. If a relation is asymmetric and ⟨d, e⟩ is in the relation, then ⟨e, d⟩ cannot be in the relation. The pair ⟨France, France⟩ is in the relation, but the pair with its elements reversed, that is, ⟨France, France⟩ (which happens to be the same ordered pair again), is in the relation as well, thereby violating the condition for asymmetry.

In the diagram of an asymmetric relation there are only 'one-way' arrows: there is never an arrow from an object d to an object e and then an arrow back from e to d. This implies that in the diagram of an asymmetric relation there cannot be any loops, because if there is an arrow from d to d, there is also, trivially, an arrow 'back' from d to d: the very same arrow.

The relation in the diagram on page 10 is antisymmetric: in an antisymmetric relation there must not be two different objects with arrows in both directions between them. Thus, antisymmetry is the same as asymmetry except that in an antisymmetric relation elements may have loops attached to them. In the above diagram there are objects with loops, but no two different objects with arrows in both directions between them. Therefore, the relation is antisymmetric.

I turn to another example. Consider the relation with the following diagram:

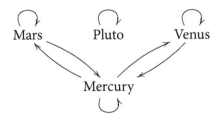

This relation is reflexive on the set {Mars, Pluto, Venus, Mercury}; it is also symmetric. It fails to be transitive since direct arrows are missing, for instance, from 'Mars' to 'Venus'. The relation is not asymmetric or antisymmetric since there are arrows going back and forth between names in the diagram, for instance between 'Mars' and 'Mercury'.

The relation ∅ has some peculiar properties: its diagram is empty. It is reflexive on the empty set ∅, but on no other set. It is symmetric, as there is no arrow for which there is not any arrow in the opposite direction. But it is also asymmetric and antisymmetric because there is no arrow for which there is an arrow in the opposite direction. ∅ is also transitive.

The relation with the diagram below is not reflexive on the set with the two elements Ponte Vecchio and Eiffel Tower, because there is no loop attached to 'Eiffel Tower'.

Eiffel Tower ⇄ Ponte Vecchio

The relation is symmetric, but not asymmetric or antisymmetric. It is also not transitive: there is an arrow from 'Eiffel Tower' to 'Ponte Vecchio' and an arrow back from 'Ponte Vecchio' to 'Eiffel Tower', but there is no short cut from 'Eiffel Tower' directly to 'Eiffel Tower', that is, there is no loop attached to 'Eiffel Tower'.

Now I turn to a relation that cannot easily be described by a diagram or by listing the pairs in the relation, namely to the relation that obtains between persons d and e if and only if d is at least as tall as e, that is, the relation that contains exactly those pairs $\langle d, e \rangle$ such that d is at least as tall as e. This relation is reflexive on the set of all persons because every person is at least as tall as themselves. The relation is not symmetric: I am taller than my brother, so I am at least as tall as he is, but he is not at least as tall as I am. Thus the pair ⟨Volker Halbach, Volker Halbach's brother⟩ is an element of the relation, while ⟨Volker Halbach's brother, Volker Halbach⟩ is not an element of the relation. The relation is transitive: if d is at least as tall as e and e is at least as tall as f, then surely d is at least as tall as f.

The relation of *loving* contains exactly those ordered pairs ⟨d, e⟩ such that d loves e. This relation is presumably not reflexive on the set of all persons: some people do not love themselves. Much grief is caused by the fact that this relation is not symmetric, and the fortunate cases of mutual love show that the relation is also not asymmetric or antisymmetric. It clearly fails to be transitive: there are many cases in which d loves e and e loves f, but in many cases d does not love his or her rival f.

The relation of *not having the same hair colour* is the set containing exactly those pairs ⟨d, e⟩ such that d does not have the same hair colour as e. This relation is surely not reflexive on the set of all persons, but it is symmetric: if d's hair colour is different from e's hair colour, then surely e's hair colour is different from d's hair colour. The relation fails to be transitive: my hair colour is different from my brother's hair colour and his hair colour is different from mine. If the relation were transitive, then I would have a hair colour that differs from my own hair colour. More formally, the pairs ⟨Volker Halbach, Volker Halbach's brother⟩ and ⟨Volker Halbach's brother, Volker Halbach⟩ are in the relation, while ⟨Volker Halbach, Volker Halbach⟩ is not. This example illustrates again that in the definition of transitivity it is not presupposed that d must be different from f.

The relation of being born on the same day is reflexive, symmetric, and transitive on the set of all persons. Persons stand in the relation of being born on the same day if and only if they are born on the same day, that is, if they are equal or equivalent with respect to their birthday. Hence the relation expresses some kind of equivalence and such relations are known as equivalence relations.

DEFINITION 1.4. *A binary relation R is an equivalence relation on S iff R is reflexive on S, symmetric on S and transitive on S.*

As before, the restriction 'on S' expresses that only elements of S are taken into account.

I will now turn to another very important kind of relation. It is so important that it deserves a section of its own.

1.3 FUNCTIONS

DEFINITION 1.5. *A binary relation R is a function iff for all d, e, f: if $\langle d, e \rangle \in R$ and $\langle d, f \rangle \in R$ then $e = f$.*

Thus a relation is a function if for every d there is at most one e such that $\langle d, e \rangle$ is in the relation.

In the diagram of a function there is at most one arrow leaving from any point in the diagram. In order to illustrate this, I will consider the function with the following four ordered pairs as its elements:

$\langle$France, Paris$\rangle$

$\langle$Italy, Rome$\rangle$

$\langle$England, London$\rangle$

$\langle$the United Kingdom, London$\rangle$

The function has the following diagram:

France ⟶ Paris

Italy ⟶ Rome

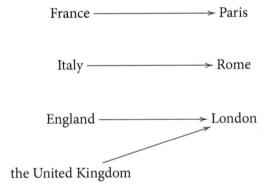

England ⟶ London

the United Kingdom

In this diagram, there are arrows from 'France', 'Italy', 'England', and 'the United Kingdom'. The set containing France, Italy, England, and the United Kingdom is called 'the domain' of the function. The names of the three cities receive arrows; the set of these three cities is called 'the range' of the function.

DEFINITION 1.6.

  (i) *The domain of a function R is the set { d: there is an e such that $\langle d, e \rangle \in R$ }.*

  (ii) *The range of a function R is the set { e: there is a d such that $\langle d, e \rangle \in R$ }.*

  (iii) *R is a function into the set S if and only if all elements of the range of the function are in S.*

The elements of the domain serve as 'inputs' or 'arguments' of the function; the elements of the range are 'outputs' or 'values'.

In the above example the set containing France, Italy, England, and the United Kingdom is the domain of the function, while the set with Paris, Rome, and London as its elements is the range. According to (iii) of the above definition, the function is a function into the set of all European cities, for instance.

DEFINITION 1.7. *If d is in the domain of a function R one writes $R(d)$ for the unique object e such that $\langle d, e \rangle$ is in R.*

The relation containing all pairs $\langle d, e \rangle$ such that d has e as a biological mother is a function: if d has e as biological mother and d has f as biological mother, then e and f must be identical. Its domain is the set of all people and animals, its range the set of all female animals with offspring.

In contrast, the relation containing all pairs $\langle d, e \rangle$ such that d is the biological mother of e is not a function: my brother and I have the same biological mother, yet we are not identical.

1.4 NON-BINARY RELATIONS

The relations I have considered so far are binary; they contain only ordered pairs. Expressions such as '*d* loves *e*' express binary relations; the expression '*d* loves *e*' expresses the relation that contains exactly those ordered pairs $\langle d, e \rangle$ such that *d* loves *e*. In contrast, the expression '*d* prefers *e* over *f*' expresses a ternary (3-place) relation rather than a binary one. In order to deal with ternary relations, ordered triples (or 'triples' for short) are used. Triples are very much like ordered pairs.

A triple $\langle d, e, f \rangle$ is identical with a triple $\langle g, h, i \rangle$ if and only if they agree in the first, second, and third component, respectively, that is, if and only if $d = g$, $e = h$, and $f = i$.[7]

Ternary relations are sets containing only triples.

Besides ordered pairs and triples there are also quadruples and so on. This can be generalized to even higher 'arities' *n*: an *n*-tuple

$$\langle d_1, d_2, \ldots, d_n \rangle$$

has *n* components.

An *n*-tuple $\langle d_1, d_2, \ldots, d_n \rangle$ and an *n*-tuple $\langle e_1, e_2, \ldots, e_n \rangle$ are identical if and only if $d_1 = e_1$ and $d_2 = e_2$ and so on up to $d_n = e_n$. Now *n*-tuples allow one to deal with *n*-place relations:

An n-place relation is a set containing only n-tuples. An n-place relation is called a relation of arity n.

For instance, there is the relation that contains exactly those 5-tuples $\langle d, e, f, g, h \rangle$ such that *d* killed *e* with *f* in *g* with the help of *h*. This is a 5-ary relation, which, for instance, contains among others the 5-tuple $\langle$ Brutus, Caesar, Brutus' knife, Rome, Cassius $\rangle$.

I also allow 1-tuples as a special case. I stipulate that $\langle d \rangle$ is simply *d* itself. Thus a 1-place or unary relation is just some set.

---

7 As has been remarked in footnote 6 above, one can define ordered pairs as certain sets. Similarly one can define the triple $\langle d, e, f \rangle$ using ordered pairs as $\langle \langle d, e \rangle, f \rangle$. So in the end only sets are needed.

1.5 ARGUMENTS, VALIDITY, AND CONTRADICTIONS

In logic usually sentences are taken as the objects that can be true or false. Of course not every sentence of English can be true or false: a command or a question is neither true nor false.

Sentences that are true or false are called declarative sentences. In what follows I will focus exclusively on declarative sentences. I will often drop the restriction 'declarative', because I will be concerned exclusively with declarative sentences.

Whether a sentence is true or not may depend on who is uttering the sentence, who is addressed, where it is said, and various other factors. The sentence 'I am Volker Halbach' is true when I say it, but the same sentence is false when uttered by you, the reader. 'It is raining' might be true in Oxford but false in Los Angeles at the same time. So the truth of the sentence depends partly on the context, that is, on the speaker, the place, the addressee, and so on. Dealing with contexts is tricky and logicians have developed theories about how the context relates to the truth of a sentence. I will try to use examples where the context of utterance does not really matter, but for some examples the context will matter. Even in those cases, what I am going to say will be correct as long as the context does not shift during the discussion of an example. This will guarantee that a true sentence cannot become false from one line to the other.

We often draw conclusions from certain sentences, and a sentence is often said to follow from or to be a consequence of certain sentences. Words like 'therefore', 'so', or 'hence', or phrases such as 'it follows that' often mark a sentence that is supposed to follow from one or more sentences. The sentences from which one concludes a sentence are called 'premisses', the sentence which is claimed to be supported by the premisses is called 'conclusion'. Together premisses and conclusion form an argument.

DEFINITION 1.8. *An argument consists of a set of declarative sentences (the premisses) and a declarative sentence (the conclusion) marked as the concluded sentence.*

There is no restriction on how the conclusion is marked as such. Expressions like 'therefore' or 'so' may be used for marking the conclusion. Often the conclusion is found at the end of an argument. The conclusion, however, may also be stated at the beginning of an argument and the premisses, preceded by phrases such as 'this follows from' or 'for', follow the conclusion.

In an argument there is always exactly one conclusion, but there may be arbitrarily many premisses; there may be even only one premiss or no premiss at all.

The following is an argument with the single premiss 'Zeno is a tortoise' and the conclusion 'Zeno is toothless'.

> Zeno is a tortoise. Therefore Zeno is toothless.

A biologist will probably accept that the conclusion follows from the premiss 'Zeno is a tortoise', as he will know that tortoises do not have teeth. That the conclusion follows from the premiss depends on a certain biological fact. This assumption can be made explicit by adding the premiss that tortoises are toothless. This will make the argument convincing not only to biologists but also to people with no biological knowledge at all. The biologist, if prompted for a more explicit version of the argument, would probably restate the argument with the additional premiss on which he may have implicity relied all along:

> Zeno is a tortoise. All tortoises are toothless. Therefore Zeno is toothless.

After adding this premiss, no special knowledge of the subject matter is required to see that the conclusion follows from the premisses. The conclusion follows from the two premisses purely formally or logically: the conclusion is a consequence of the premisses independently of any subject-specific assumptions. It does not matter who Zeno is, what tortoises are, what being toothless is, or which objects there are.

In this argument the conclusion follows from the premisses independently of what the premisses and conclusion are about. Whatever they are taken to be about, in whatever way the subject-specific terms are (re-)interpreted, the conclusion will be true if the premises are. Arguments of this kind are called 'logically valid' or 'formally valid'. Thus in a logically valid argument the conclusion follows from the premises independently of the subject matter.

CHARACTERIZATION 1.9 (LOGICAL VALIDITY). *An argument is logically valid if and only if there is no interpretation under which the premisses are all true and the conclusion is false.*[8]

In particular, if all terms are interpreted in the standard way, then, according to Characterization 1.9, the conclusion is true if the premisses are true. Thus the conclusion of a logically valid argument is true if the premises are true.

The notion of an interpretation employed in Characterization 1.9 needs some clarification: An interpretation will assign meanings to the subject-specific terms such as 'Zeno', 'tortoise', and 'iridium'. It will also determine which objects the argument is taken to be about. The logical terms, that is, the subject-independent terms such as 'all', are not subject to any (re-)interpretation. These logical terms belong to the form of the argument and they are not affected by interpretations.

In later chapters I shall provide an exact definition of interpretations or 'structures', as I shall call them in the case of formal languages. These formal accounts of logical validity can also be seen as attempts to elucidate the notion of logical validity in natural languages such as English at least for those parts of English that can be translated into the formal languages.

According to the characterization of logical validity, the meanings of the subject-specific terms do not matter for the logical validity of the argument. Thus, one can replace these terms by other terms and thereby obtain a logically valid argument again. The following argument has

8 A precise and informative definition of the logical validity of a argument is not so easy to give. Sainsbury (2001, chapter 1) provides a critical introductory discussion.

been obtained from the argument about Zeno by such a substitution of non-logical, that is, subject-specific terms:

> Iridium is a metal. All metals are chemical elements. Therefore iridium is a chemical element.

Both the argument about Zeno and the argument about iridium have the same pattern; they share the same form. The conclusion follows from the premisses solely in virtue of the form of the argument. This is the reason for calling such arguments 'formally valid'.

The notion of logical or formal validity is occasionally contrasted with other, less strict notions of validity, under which more arguments come out as valid. Some arguments in which the truth of the premisses does guarantee the truth of the conclusion are not formally valid. Here is an example:

> Hagen is a bachelor. Therefore Hagen is not married.

In this argument the conclusion is bound to be true if the premiss is true, but it is not logically or formally valid, that is, valid in virtue of its form. 'Hagen is not married' follows from 'Hagen is a bachelor' in virtue of the meaning of the word 'bachelor', which is subject-specific.

Also, arguments in which the premisses do not guarantee the truth of the conclusion are often called valid. Here is an example:

> All emeralds observed so far have been green. Therefore all emeralds are green.

The premiss may support the conclusion in some sense, but it does not guarantee the truth of the conclusion. Such arguments as the argument above are said to be inductively valid. *In logically valid arguments, in contrast, the truth of the premisses guarantees the truth of the conclusion. Logically valid arguments are also called 'deductively valid'.*

In this book I will focus on logical validity and not consider other, less stringent kinds of validity. Therefore, I shall often drop the specification 'logical' or 'formal': validity will always be understood as logical validity.

There are good reasons to focus on logically valid arguments. Philosophers often suppress premisses in arguments because they think that these premisses are too obvious to state. However, one philosopher's obvious premiss can be another philosopher's very contentious premiss. Trying to make an argument logically valid forces one to make all hidden assumptions explicit. This may unearth premisses that are not obvious and uncontroversial at all. Also, there is usually not a unique way to add premisses to render an argument logically valid, and it may remain controversial which premisses were implicitly assumed by the original author, or whether he relied on any implicit premisses at all. At any rate, if an argument is formally valid, then the validity does not rely on any potentially controversial subject-specific assumptions: all the assumptions needed to establish the conclusion will be explicitly laid out for inspection.

This is not to say that logical validity is always obvious: all required premisses may have been made explicit, but it might not be obvious that the conclusion follows from the premisses, that is, one might not be able to see easily that the argument is logically valid. Characterization 1.9 of logical validity does not demand an obvious connection between the premisses and the conclusion that is easy to grasp. Almost all of the examples of logically valid arguments considered in this book are toy examples where it will be fairly obvious that they are logically valid, but showing that an argument is logically valid can be extremely difficult. Mathematicians, for instance, are mainly concerned with establishing that certain sentences (theorems) follow from certain premisses (axioms), that is, with showing that certain arguments are logically valid. Of course one can try to break up valid arguments into chains of short and obvious steps. In Chapter 6 this task is taken up and a formal notion of proof is developed.

A valid argument need not have a true conclusion. In the following example the non-logical terms of the logically valid argument about Zeno (or iridium) have been replaced in such a way as to make the conclusion false:

> Water is a metal. All metals are chemical elements. There-
> fore water is a chemical element.

Although the conclusion 'Water is a chemical element' is false, the argument is logically valid: the conclusion still follows from the premisses.
In a logically valid argument the conclusion may be false as long as at
least one premiss is false. In this case 'Water is a metal' is false. Therefore, one cannot refute the validity of an argument by merely pointing
out a false conclusion. If the conclusion of an argument is false, then either at least one of the premisses is false or the argument is not logically
valid (or both).

So far I have used only one argument form (argument pattern) in
my examples. Here is an argument of a different pattern:

> Either CO_2-emissions are being cut or there will be more
> floods. It is not the case that CO_2-emissions are being cut.
> Therefore there will be more floods.

The argument is logically valid according to Characterization 1.9 of logically valid arguments since the validity of the argument does not depend on the subject-specific terms such as 'CO_2-emissions' and 'floods'.
The validity of the argument depends on the logical terms 'either ... or
...' and 'it is not the case that ...'.

In the argument about Zeno I could replace various terms, but not
complete sentences. In the present example one can replace entire sentences. In this case the argument will still be valid after replacing the
sentences 'CO_2-emissions are being cut' and 'There will be more floods'
with some other sentences. The pattern of the valid argument is a pattern of whole sentences. Valid arguments of this kind are said to be
propositionally valid. Thus an argument is propositionally valid if and
only if there is no (re-)interpretation of the sentences in the argument
such that all premisses are true and yet the conclusion is false. These
patterns of propositionally valid arguments are studied in sentential or
propositional logic. Propositional validity will be treated in Chapters 2
and 3.

The argument about Zeno can be adequately analysed in predicate logic only, and not in propositional logic. Predicate logic is based on propositional logic; from the technical point of view it is a refinement of propositional logic. Thus I shall start with propositional logic and then move on to predicate logic.

The notion of logical consistency, or just consistency for short, is closely related to the notion of validity.

CHARACTERIZATION 1.10 (CONSISTENCY). *A set of sentences is logically consistent if and only if there is a least one interpretation under which all sentences of the set are true.*

The negation of a sentence is obtained by writing 'It is not the case that' in front of the sentence (in English there are various stylistically more elegant ways to express negation). 'It is not the case that' should be understood as pertaining to the entire original sentence. A sentence is false if and only if its negation is true.

For a valid argument there is no interpretation under which the premisses are all true and the conclusion is false. Thus, for a valid argument there is no interpretation under which the premisses are all true and the negation of the conclusion is also true. Thus, if an argument is valid, the set obtained by adding the negation of the conclusion to the premisses is not consistent (or inconsistent, for short); and if the set obtained by adding the negation of the conclusion to the premisses is inconsistent, then there is no interpretation under which all sentences of that set are true, and, consequently, there is no interpretation under which all the premisses are true and the conclusion is false. Hence one can define validity in terms of consistency: *An argument is valid if and only if the set obtained by adding the negation of the conclusion to the premisses is inconsistent.*

I have not imposed any restrictions on the number of premisses in an argument. In particular, there may be no premisses at all. Arguments with no premisses may still be logically valid. The following argument does not have any premisses but only a conclusion:

All metaphysicians are metaphysicians.

The sentence is true, and it is true for any interpretation of 'metaphysician', which is the only non-logical, subject-specific term in the sentence. Therefore, there is no interpretation under which all premisses are true (there is none) and the conclusion is false. Therefore, the argument is logically valid. The conclusion of a logically valid argument with no premisses is also called 'logically true' or 'logically valid'.

CHARACTERIZATION 1.11 (LOGICAL TRUTH). *A sentence is logically true if and only if it is true under any interpretation.*

There are also sentences that cannot be made true by any interpretation. These sentences are called 'logically false'. They are called 'logical contradictions' or just contradictions.

CHARACTERIZATION 1.12 (CONTRADICTION). *A sentence is a contradiction if and only if it is false under all interpretations.*

If a sentence *A* follows logically from a sentence *B* and *B* follows logically from *A*, that is, if the argument with *A* as its only premiss and *B* as conclusion, and the argument with *B* as premiss and *A* as conclusion, are logically valid, then the sentences *A* and *B* are logically equivalent. According to Characterization 1.9, the argument with *A* as premiss and *B* as conclusion and the argument with *B* as premiss and *A* as conclusion are both logically valid if and only if *A* and *B* are true under the same interpretations:

CHARACTERIZATION 1.13 (LOGICAL EQUIVALENCE). *Sentences are logically equivalent if and only if they are true under exactly the same interpretations.*

1.6 SYNTAX, SEMANTICS, AND PRAGMATICS

In the following chapters I will examine formal languages. These languages are in many respects much less complicated than natural languages such as English or German. They are intended to mirror certain properties of natural languages. Some philosophers conceive of these formal languages as models for natural languages.

Usually, in analysing either natural or formal languages one distinguishes three aspects of a language: syntax, semantics, and pragmatics.[9] In order to use a language competently, one must master all three aspects of it.

Syntax is concerned with the expressions of a language bare of their meanings. In the syntax of a language it is specified what the words or sentences of the language are. In general, the grammar of a language belongs to the syntax of that language, and often syntax is identified with grammar. In order to use the language competently, one must know the grammar of the language. In particular, one must know how to form sentences in the language.

Semantics may be described as the study of the meanings of the expressions of a language. Clearly, to use a language one must not only know what the words and the sentences of the language are; one must also know what they mean.

The expression 'Im Mondschein hockt auf den Gräbern eine wild gespenstische Gestalt' is a well-formed German declarative sentence. In a syntactic analysis of that sentence one may remark that 'hockt' is a verb in present tense, and so on. All this is merely syntactic information; it does not tell one anything about the meaning of that sentence. In order to understand the sentence, one needs information about meaning. For instance, it is a semantic fact of German that 'im Mondschein' means 'in the moonlight'.

The third component, pragmatics, will not be studied here. Pragmatics is, roughly speaking, the study of language in use. Assume John calls Mary and asks her whether she wants to come along to the cinema. She replies, 'I am ill.' Obviously, John should not expect Mary to come along, but the sentence 'I am ill' does not mean the same thing as 'I don't want to come along to the cinema'; the former sentence only says something about Mary's health. But uttered by Mary in this particular situation, the sentence 'I am ill', spoken by Mary, conveys the informa-

9 The trichotomy was introduced by Morris (1938).

tion that she will not join John. Thus, John needs pragmatics in order to understand that Mary is not going to come along. Pure semantics would not tell him.

2 Syntax and Semantics of Propositional Logic

In this chapter I shall introduce the language of propositional logic. All other formal languages that will be discussed in this manual are based on the language of propositional logic.

Before introducing the syntax of this language I will briefly outline a method for talking efficiently about the expressions of a language and for describing the syntax of a language. The method is by no means specific to the language of propositional logic.

2.1 QUOTATION

By enclosing an expression in quotation marks one can talk about that expression. Using quotation marks one can say, for instance, that 'A' is the first letter of the alphabet and that 'Gli enigmi sono tre' is an Italian sentence. The quotation of an expression is that very expression enclosed in quotation marks.[1]

Quotation marks allow one to designate, that is, to refer to single expressions. Describing the syntax of a language usually makes it necessary to talk about a large or infinite number of expressions. For instance, one would like to be able to state that one can construct new sentences in English by combining sentences using 'and' (ignoring capitalization and punctuation). Logicians would express that general claim by saying the following:

(AND) If ϕ and ψ are English sentences then 'ϕ and ψ' is an English sentence.

---

1 Cappelen and LePore (2009) provide an overview of the intricacies of quotation and of proposed theories. A classical text on quotation is Quine (1940).

'It is raining' is an English sentence. If one takes 'It is raining' as both ϕ and ψ in the above rule, then the rule says that 'It is raining and it is raining' is also an English sentence (again we ignore the absence of the full stop and the missing capitalization). One can then use 'It is raining and it is raining' as ϕ again and 'It is raining' as ψ to conclude from the rule that also 'It is raining and it is raining and it is raining' is an English sentence. In this way one can construct longer and longer sentences and there is no limit to the iterations.

I think that (AND) is fairly straightforward and should be easy to understand. There is, however, something puzzling about it as well: the part of (AND) claiming that 'ϕ and ψ' is an English sentence is decidedly not about the expression in quotation marks. The letters ϕ and ψ are Greek letters, and the expression with 'ϕ' as first symbol, followed by a space, followed by 'and' and another space, followed by 'ψ', is definitely not an English sentence. Only once 'ϕ' and 'ψ' are replaced by English sentences does 'ϕ and ψ' become an English sentence.

The Greek letters used in this way are metavariables or metalinguistic variables.

Thus, the above rule may also be expressed in the following way:

> An English sentence followed by 'and' (in spaces) and another or the same English sentence is also an English sentence.

This way of rephrasing (AND) does not rely on quotation marks but on talking about expressions following one another. This method is perhaps safer than using (AND) with its quotation marks and metavariables, but it is also more cumbersome when applied to intricate grammatical rules. Thus, I will present definitions in the style of (AND) rather than talking about expressions following one another.

Logicians hardly ever use the expressions of formal languages in the way they use the expressions of their mother tongue, but they often talk and write about the expressions of these formal languages. Since

the expressions of the formal languages they are concerned with differ from expressions of English, logicians usually drop the quotation
marks. Instead of saying

> '$(P \rightarrow (Q \wedge R))$' is a sentence of the language of proposi-
> tional logic

they say,

> $(P \rightarrow (Q \wedge R))$ is a sentence of the language of proposi-
> tional logic.

I will follow this convention and usually drop quotation marks around
the expressions of formal languages in this manual. This also applies to
expressions containing metavariables.

2.2 THE SYNTAX OF THE LANGUAGE OF PROPOSITIONAL LOGIC

Now I can describe the syntax of the language $\mathcal{L}_1$ of propositional logic.

DEFINITION 2.1 (SENTENCE LETTERS). *P, Q, R, P_1, Q_1, R_1, P_2, Q_2, R_2, P_3, Q_3, R_3, and so on are sentence letters.*

Using metavariables I will define the notion of a sentence of the
language $\mathcal{L}_1$ of propositional logic.

DEFINITION 2.2 (SENTENCE OF $\mathcal{L}_1$).

  (i) *All sentence letters are sentences of $\mathcal{L}_1$.*
 (ii) *If ϕ and ψ are sentences of $\mathcal{L}_1$, then $\neg\phi$, $(\phi \wedge \psi)$, $(\phi \vee \psi)$, $(\phi \rightarrow \psi)$ and $(\phi \leftrightarrow \psi)$ are sentences of $\mathcal{L}_1$.*
(iii) *Nothing else is a sentence of $\mathcal{L}_1$.*

Given what I have said about metavariables, (ii) implies that the expression '$(\phi \wedge \psi)$' becomes a sentence of the language of propositional
logic when the Greek letters 'ϕ' and 'ψ' have been replaced by sentences
of the language of propositional logic. The Greek letters 'ϕ' and 'ψ'
themselves are not expressions of the language $\mathcal{L}_1$.

As I explained on page 28, I could have formulated part (ii) of Definition 2.2 without using the metavariables 'ϕ' and 'ψ' by expressing (ii) in the following way:

> The negation symbol followed by a sentence of $\mathcal{L}_1$ is again a sentence of $\mathcal{L}_1$. The symbol '(' followed by a sentence of $\mathcal{L}_1$, followed by the symbol '$\vee$' (or '$\wedge$', '$\rightarrow$', '$\leftrightarrow$'), followed by a sentence (not necessarily distinct from the first one), followed by the symbol ')', is a sentence of $\mathcal{L}_1$.

I hope that (ii) is not only shorter but also easier to grasp.

The last clause in Definition 2.2 says that only expressions one can obtain by using clauses (i) and (ii) are sentences. Very often this last clause is omitted and the clauses (i) and (ii) are implicitly taken to be the only means of arriving at sentences. At various points in this manual I will provide definitions that are similar to Definition 2.2. In those cases I will drop the analogues of clause (iii) for the sake of simplicity.

Logicians also say 'the negation of ϕ' rather than '$\neg\phi$'. *In this terminology, $\neg\phi$ is the negation of ϕ, and similarly $(\phi \wedge \psi)$ is the conjunction of ϕ and ψ, and $(\phi \vee \psi)$ is the disjunction of ϕ and ψ.* The sentence $\neg(P \rightarrow Q)$, for instance, is the negation of $(P \rightarrow Q)$.

EXAMPLE 2.3. The following expressions are sentences of the language $\mathcal{L}_1$:

$$((P \rightarrow P) \wedge Q_{456}),$$
$$\neg(R \vee (P \vee (P_3 \vee \neg Q_4))),$$
$$((\neg P \wedge Q_4) \rightarrow P).$$

In the next example I show how to prove that the last sentence above is indeed a sentence of $\mathcal{L}_1$.

EXAMPLE 2.4. By Definition 2.2(i), P is a sentence of $\mathcal{L}_1$. Thus, by (ii), $\neg P$ is also a sentence of $\mathcal{L}_1$. By (i) again, Q_4 is a sentence of $\mathcal{L}_1$. By (ii) and by what has been said so far, $(\neg P \wedge Q_4)$ is a sentence, and by (ii) again and by what has been said so far, $((\neg P \wedge Q_4) \rightarrow P)$ is also a sentence of $\mathcal{L}_1$.

The symbols ¬, ∧, ∨, →, ↔ *are called 'connectives'.* They roughly correspond to the English expressions 'not', 'and', 'or', 'if …, then …' and 'if and only if', respectively.

name	in English	symbol used here	alternative symbols
conjunction	and	∧	., &
disjunction	or	∨	+, v
negation	it is not the case that	¬	−, ~
arrow (material implication, conditional)	if … then	→	⊃, ⇒
double arrow, (biconditional material equivalence)	if and only if	↔	≡, ⇔

The names in brackets and the symbols in the rightmost column are used by some other authors; they will not be used here.

The expressions in the 'in English' column indicate how the connectives are commonly read, rather than their precise meanings.

2.3 RULES FOR DROPPING BRACKETS

A sentence with many brackets can be confusing. For convenience I shall employ certain rules for dropping brackets. These rules are not revisions of the definition of a sentence and they do not form part of the official syntax of the language $\mathcal{L}_1$ of propositional logic. These rules are mere conventions that allow one to write down abbreviations of sentences instead of the sentences themselves in their official form.

Most logicians employ at least some of these rules. For instance, hardly anyone writes $(P \wedge Q)$ instead of $P \wedge Q$. This, then, is the first rule:

BRACKETING CONVENTION 1. *The outer brackets may be omitted from a sentence that is not part of another sentence.*

For instance, one may write $P \to (Q \vee P)$ instead of $(P \to (Q \vee P))$. However, this convention does not allow one to drop any brackets from $\neg(P \to (Q \vee P))$, because the sentence $(P \to (Q \vee P))$ is written here as a part of the sentence $\neg(P \to (Q \vee P))$.

One has to be cautious here. The syntactic definitions in Section 2.2 apply to $\mathcal{L}_1$-sentences but not to their abbreviations. For instance, I have defined the negation of the sentence ϕ as $\neg\phi$. Now one might think that $\neg P \wedge Q$ is the negation of $P \wedge Q$. This is not the case, however. $P \wedge Q$ is short for $(P \wedge Q)$ according to Convention 1; and the negation of $(P \wedge Q)$ is $\neg(P \wedge Q)$ and not $\neg P \wedge Q$, which is short for $(\neg P \wedge Q)$.

BRACKETING CONVENTION 2. *The inner set of brackets may be omitted from a sentence of the form $((\phi \wedge \psi) \wedge \chi)$. An analogous convention applies to $\vee$.*

By this convention $((P \wedge Q_2) \wedge P_2)$ can be abbreviated as $(P \wedge Q_2 \wedge P_2)$.

The bracketing conventions can be combined and all pairs of brackets that can be dropped in accordance with some convention may be omitted from a sentence. For instance, in the sentence $((P \wedge Q_2) \wedge P_2)$ above, the outer pair of brackets may be dropped by Convention 1, and the inner pair of brackets may be dropped by Convention 2. So $P \wedge Q_2 \wedge P_2$ is also an abbreviation of $((P \wedge Q_2) \wedge P_2)$.

Convention 2 applies even when $((\phi \wedge \psi) \wedge \chi)$ forms part of a larger sentence. So, using Conventions 1 and 2, one can abbreviate the sentence

$$((((P_2 \wedge P_3) \wedge Q) \wedge R) \to ((P_2 \vee \neg P_3) \vee Q))$$

with the following expression:

$$(P_2 \wedge P_3 \wedge Q \wedge R) \to (P_2 \vee \neg P_3 \vee Q).$$

In arithmetic one may write $3 \times 5 + 4$ instead of $(3 \times 5) + 4$, because the symbol $\times$ for multiplication binds more strongly than the symbol $+$ for

addition. Analogously, there are conventions for ordering logical oper-
ations: $\wedge$ and $\vee$ bind more strongly than $\to$ or $\leftrightarrow$. And just as in the case
of arithmetic, this yields further conventions for dropping brackets.

For instance, the sentence $P \leftrightarrow Q \wedge R$ is in abbreviated form. In order to decide whether the sentence is an abbreviation of $((P \leftrightarrow Q) \wedge R)$
or of $(P \leftrightarrow (Q \wedge R))$, imagine that the connectives $\leftrightarrow$ and $\wedge$ 'compete'
for the sentence letter Q. Since $\wedge$ binds more strongly than $\leftrightarrow$, $\wedge$ gains
the upper hand and $(P \leftrightarrow (Q \wedge R))$ is the correct reading.

In more abstract terms, this rule for dropping brackets can be expressed as follows:

BRACKETING CONVENTION 3. *Assume ϕ, ψ, and χ are sentences of $\mathcal{L}_1$,
$\diamond$ is either $\wedge$ or $\vee$, and $\circ$ is either $\to$ or $\leftrightarrow$. Then, if $(\phi \circ (\psi \diamond \chi))$ or
$((\phi \diamond \psi) \circ \chi)$ occurs as part of the sentence that is to be abbreviated, the
inner set of brackets may be omitted.*

After dropping the outer brackets from $((P \wedge Q) \to R)$ according
to Convention 1, one may shorten the sentence further to $P \wedge Q \to R$
since $\wedge$ binds more strongly than $\to$. Similarly $\neg(P \to ((Q \wedge P_3) \vee R))$
may be abbreviated as $\neg(P \to (Q \wedge P_3) \vee R)$. In $(\neg(P \vee Q) \leftrightarrow Q)$
only the outer brackets can be omitted in virtue of Convention 1, so
that $\neg(P \vee Q) \leftrightarrow Q$ is obtained as an abbreviation. One cannot use
Convention 3 to obtain $\neg P \vee Q \leftrightarrow Q$, because the original sentence
does not contain $((P \vee Q) \leftrightarrow Q)$ as a part. Intuitively, in $\neg P \vee Q \leftrightarrow Q$
the negation symbol $\neg$ applies only to P and not to the sentence $(P \vee Q)$
as it does in the original sentence.

There is no deeper reason for the choice of these three conventions.
It is never incorrect to use the unabbreviated sentences of $\mathcal{L}_1$ with all
their brackets rather than their abbreviations. In situations where the
application of the bracketing conventions can give rise to confusions,
it is better not to use them. Also it is perfectly legitimate to apply the
rules selectively. For instance, one may apply only Convention 1, but
not Convention 3, and write $(P \wedge Q) \to R$ for $((P \wedge Q) \to R)$. I will
apply these conventions extensively.

2.4 THE SEMANTICS OF PROPOSITIONAL LOGIC

In Section 1.5 I gave a characterization of the logical validity of arguments in English. In this section I will define validity for arguments in the language $\mathcal{L}_1$ of propositional logic. The informal Characterization 1.9 of validity for English arguments will be adapted to the language $\mathcal{L}_1$ of propositional logic and thereby be transformed into a precise definition.

In order to define logical validity for the language $\mathcal{L}_1$, the notion of an interpretation for the language $\mathcal{L}_1$ needs to be made precise. First, I need to say which expressions can be interpreted in different ways and which are always interpreted in the same way. The connectives are logical symbols, the brackets merely auxiliary symbols; logical and auxiliary symbols cannot be reinterpreted (insofar as one can speak of auxiliary symbols' being interpreted at all). The sentence letters are the only non-logical symbols of $\mathcal{L}_1$; they can be interpreted in different ways.

The interpretations of the sentence letters will be provided by so-called $\mathcal{L}_1$-structures. These $\mathcal{L}_1$-structures need only provide enough information to determine whether a sentence is true or false. Now, under what conditions is the sentence $P \wedge Q$ true? If the connective $\wedge$ functions like 'and' in English, then both P and Q must be true for $P \wedge Q$ to be true; otherwise $P \wedge Q$ will be false. Similarly, since $\neg$ works like 'not', the sentence $\neg R$ is true if and only if R is false. As $\vee$ corresponds to 'or', the sentence $P \vee Q$ is true if and only if P or Q is true (or both are true).

The arrow $\rightarrow$ corresponds roughly to the English 'if ... then', but the latter has a rather complicated semantics. The $\mathcal{L}_1$-sentence $P \rightarrow Q$ is false if and only if P is true and Q is false; otherwise it is true. The phrase 'if ... then', which corresponds to the arrow, does *not* always behave like this. How the arrow $\rightarrow$ is related to 'if ... then' will be discussed in Section 3.1.

In $\mathcal{L}_1$ the truth or falsity of a sentence of $\mathcal{L}_1$ depends always only on the truth or falsity of the sentence letters occurring in the sentence (and the connectives in the sentence); any further information contained in the sentences is not relevant. Therefore, $\mathcal{L}_1$-structures need only determine the truth and falsity of all sentence letters.

Instead of saying that a sentence is true, logicians say that the sentence has the truth-value True. This sounds like a philosophically profound move since new objects are required: truth-values. Truth-values, however, are hardly mysterious objects. In the end it matters only that True and False are distinct; and some more mathematically minded logicians use the number 1 for the truth-value True and 0 for the truth-value False.

It is possible, although not very customary and technically less convenient, to develop the semantics of $\mathcal{L}_1$ without truth-values by saying that a sentence is true (or false) instead of saying that it has the truth-value True (or False). I shall use the letter 'T' as a name for the truth-value True and 'F' for the truth-value False.

Thus an $\mathcal{L}_1$-structure provides interpretations of all sentence letters by assigning to every sentence letter exactly one truth-value, T or F.

DEFINITION 2.5 ($\mathcal{L}_1$-STRUCTURE). *An $\mathcal{L}_1$-structure is an assignment of exactly one truth-value (T or F) to every sentence letter of $\mathcal{L}_1$.*[2]

One may think of an $\mathcal{L}_1$-structure as an infinite list that provides a value T or F for every sentence letter. The beginning of such a list could look like this:

P	Q	R	P_1	Q_1	R_1	P_2	Q_2	R_2	
T	F	F	F	T	F	T	T	F	...

Starting from the truth-values assigned to the sentence letters by an $\mathcal{L}_1$-structure $\mathcal{A}$, one can work out the truth-values for sentences containing connectives in the following way. The shortest sentences are the sentence letters; their respective truth-values are fixed directly by the $\mathcal{L}_1$-structure $\mathcal{A}$. For instance, P could be assigned the truth-value T and R could be assigned the same truth-value. In this case $P \wedge R$ would

---

2 In more mathematical terms, an $\mathcal{L}_1$-structure is a function into the set $\{T, F\}$ with the set of all sentence letters of $\mathcal{L}_1$ as its domain.

receive the truth-value T, too. If P_1 is given the truth-value F by $\mathcal{A}$, the sentence $P_1 \vee (P \wedge R)$ gets the truth-value T, because $P \wedge R$ is true; and ψ's being true is sufficient to make a sentence $\phi \vee \psi$ true.

Thus, the truth-values of the shortest sentences, that is, of the sentence letters, are fixed by the $\mathcal{L}_1$-structure $\mathcal{A}$, and then the truth-values for longer sentences are determined successively by the truth-values of the sentences they are made up from.

I will write $|\phi|_{\mathcal{A}}$ for the truth-value of ϕ that is obtained on the basis of $\mathcal{A}$; it is determined by $\mathcal{A}$ in the following way:

DEFINITION 2.6 (TRUTH IN AN $\mathcal{L}_1$-STRUCTURE).
Let $\mathcal{A}$ be some $\mathcal{L}_1$-structure. Then $|\ldots|_{\mathcal{A}}$ assigns either T or F to every sentence of $\mathcal{L}_1$ in the following way:[3]

   (i) *If ϕ is a sentence letter, $|\phi|_{\mathcal{A}}$ is the truth-value assigned to ϕ by the $\mathcal{L}_1$-structure $\mathcal{A}$.*
   (ii) *$|\neg\phi|_{\mathcal{A}} = T$ if and only if $|\phi|_{\mathcal{A}} = F$.*
   (iii) *$|\phi \wedge \psi|_{\mathcal{A}} = T$ if and only if $|\phi|_{\mathcal{A}} = T$ and $|\psi|_{\mathcal{A}} = T$.*
   (iv) *$|\phi \vee \psi|_{\mathcal{A}} = T$ if and only if $|\phi|_{\mathcal{A}} = T$ or $|\psi|_{\mathcal{A}} = T$.*
   (v) *$|\phi \to \psi|_{\mathcal{A}} = T$ if and only if $|\phi|_{\mathcal{A}} = F$ or $|\psi|_{\mathcal{A}} = T$.*
   (vi) *$|\phi \leftrightarrow \psi|_{\mathcal{A}} = T$ if and only if $|\phi|_{\mathcal{A}} = |\psi|_{\mathcal{A}}$.*

Instead of writing $|\phi|_{\mathcal{A}} = T$, I will sometimes write that ϕ is true in $\mathcal{A}$ or that T is the truth-value of ϕ in $\mathcal{A}$.

The definition of $|\ldots|_{\mathcal{A}}$ does not say explicitly when a sentence has the truth-value F in $\mathcal{A}$. Nonetheless, extra clauses for falsity are not required, since a sentence has the truth-value F (in $\mathcal{A}$) if and only if it does not have the truth-value T. In particular, a sentence letter has the truth-value F if and only if it is not true in $\mathcal{A}$. Similarly, for negation the following falsity clause follows from Definition 2.6:

$$|\neg\phi|_{\mathcal{A}} = F \text{ if and only if } |\phi|_{\mathcal{A}} = T.$$

---

[3] More formally, $|\ldots|_{\mathcal{A}}$ is a function with the set of all $\mathcal{L}_1$-sentences as its domain into the set $\{T, F\}$. It properly extends the $\mathcal{L}_1$-structure $\mathcal{A}$, that is, it contains all the ordered pairs that the function $\mathcal{A}$ contains and more besides them.

Definition 2.6 also implies the following claim for conjunction (and similarly for the other connectives):

$$|\phi \wedge \psi|_A = \text{F} \text{ if and only if } |\phi|_A = \text{F} \text{ or } |\psi|_A = \text{F}.$$

Thus, Definition 2.6 also says whether a sentence is false in a given structure. For example, consider the sentence $(\neg(P \to Q) \to (P \wedge Q))$ and a structure $\mathcal{B}$ that assigns T to the sentence letter P and F to the sentence letter Q. I want to determine the truth-value $|\neg(P \to Q) \to (P \wedge Q)|_\mathcal{B}$. Using the various clauses of Definition 2.6, one can calculate its truth-value by calculating the truth-values of the sentences that were used in building it up according to the syntactic rules (Definition 2.2) for forming $\mathcal{L}_1$-sentences. Here is how:

1. $|P|_\mathcal{B} = \text{T}$ by assumption and Definition 2.6(i)
2. $|Q|_\mathcal{B} = \text{F}$ by assumption and Definition 2.6(i)
3. $|P \to Q|_\mathcal{B} = \text{F}$ by 1, 2, and Definition 2.6(v)
4. $|\neg(P \to Q)|_\mathcal{B} = \text{T}$ by 3 and Definition 2.6(ii)
5. $|P \wedge Q|_\mathcal{B} = \text{F}$ by 1, 2, and Definition 2.6(iii)
6. $|\neg(P \to Q) \to (P \wedge Q)|_\mathcal{B} = \text{F}$ by 4, 5, and Definition 2.6(v)

Therefore, $\neg(P \to Q) \to (P \wedge Q)$ is not true in $\mathcal{B}$.

The clauses (ii)–(vi) of Definition 2.6 can be neatly expressed by truth tables. According to (ii), for instance, a sentence $\neg\phi$ has truth-value T if and only if ϕ has truth-value F. Thus if $|\phi|_A = \text{F}$, we have $|\neg\phi|_A = \text{T}$; and if $|\phi|_A = \text{T}$, we have $|\neg\phi|_A = \text{F}$. This is expressed in the following table:

ϕ	$\neg\phi$
T	F
F	T

The clauses (iii)–(vi) correspond to the following tables respectively:

ϕ	ψ	$(\phi \wedge \psi)$
T	T	T
T	F	F
F	T	F
F	F	F

ϕ	ψ	$(\phi \vee \psi)$
T	T	T
T	F	T
F	T	T
F	F	F

ϕ	ψ	$(\phi \rightarrow \psi)$
T	T	T
T	F	F
F	T	T
F	F	T

ϕ	ψ	$(\phi \leftrightarrow \psi)$
T	T	T
T	F	F
F	T	F
F	F	T

Truth tables are also useful for calculating the truth-values of sentences with more than one connective. I will use the same example as above to show how this can be done. The first step is to write below each sentence letter the truth-value assigned to it by the $\mathcal{L}_1$-structure $\mathcal{A}$:

P	Q	$\neg$	$(P$	$\rightarrow$	$Q)$	$\rightarrow$	$(P$	$\wedge$	$Q)$
T	F		T		F		T		F

The next step is to calculate the truth-values of sentences directly built up from sentence letters according to the truth tables (in this case the tables for $\rightarrow$ and $\wedge$ are needed):

P	Q	$\neg$	$(P$	$\rightarrow$	$Q)$	$\rightarrow$	$(P$	$\wedge$	$Q)$
T	F		T	F	F		T	F	F

Then one can go on to determine the truth-values for more and more complex sentences:

P	Q	$\neg$	$(P$	$\rightarrow$	$Q)$	$\rightarrow$	$(P$	$\wedge$	$Q)$
T	F	T	T	F	F		T	F	F

Finally, one will obtain the truth-value for the entire sentence (here highlighted using boldface):

P	Q	$\neg$	$(P$	$\rightarrow$	$Q)$	$\rightarrow$	$(P$	$\wedge$	$Q)$
T	F	T	T	F	F	**F**	T	F	F

One can also use a (multi-line) truth table to work out the truth-values of a given sentence for all $\mathcal{L}_1$-structures.

In a truth table one can also work out the truth-value of the sentence $\neg(P \rightarrow Q) \rightarrow (P \wedge Q)$ in any given $\mathcal{L}_1$-structure. I employ again the sentence $\neg(P \to Q) \to (P \wedge Q)$ as an example; it contains two sentence letters. In a given structure, P can be true or false, and Q can be true or false. Thus there are four possibilities: in any given $\mathcal{L}_1$-structure, either both P and Q are true, or P is true and Q is false, or P is false and Q is true, or both sentence letters are false. These four possibilities are captured in the two leftmost columns of the truth table below. Now one can calculate the truth-values of the sentence for all four possibilities, and, thereby, for *all* $\mathcal{L}_1$-structures:

P	Q	$\neg$	$(P$	$\to$	$Q)$	$\to$	$(P$	$\wedge$	$Q)$
T	T	F	T	T	T	**T**	T	T	T
T	F	T	T	F	F	**F**	T	F	F
F	T	F	F	T	T	**T**	F	F	T
F	F	F	F	T	F	**T**	F	F	F

Again, the column with the truth-value of the entire sentence is in boldface letters. *I will call this column the main column.*

Clearly, if there are only T's in the main column of a sentence the sentence is true in all $\mathcal{L}_1$-structures; if there are only F's in the main column the sentence is false in all $\mathcal{L}_1$-structures. Thus one can use truth tables to determine whether a sentence is always true, or whether it is always false, or whether it is true in some structures and false in others.

The notion of an $\mathcal{L}_1$-structure corresponds to that of an interpretation of an English sentence in Section 1.5. In that section I also used the notion of an English sentence being true under an interpretation; this corresponds to the notion of an $\mathcal{L}_1$-sentence being true in a structure. The definitions of logical validity and logical truth in English in Characterizations 1.9 and 1.11, and other such notions can be adapted to the language $\mathcal{L}_1$ of propositional logic. The definitions are the same for $\mathcal{L}_1$ as for English, except that the informal notion of an interpretation from Section 1.5 is replaced by the technical notion of an $\mathcal{L}_1$-structure.

DEFINITION 2.7.

(i) *A sentence ϕ of $\mathcal{L}_1$ is logically true if and only if ϕ is true in all $\mathcal{L}_1$-structures.*

(ii) *A sentence ϕ of $\mathcal{L}_1$ is a contradiction if and only if ϕ is not true in any $\mathcal{L}_1$-structure.*

(iii) *A sentence ϕ and a sentence ψ are logically equivalent if and only if ϕ and ψ are true in exactly the same $\mathcal{L}_1$-structures.*

The logically true sentences of $\mathcal{L}_1$ are also called 'tautologies'.

Logical truths, contradictions, and logically equivalent sentences of $\mathcal{L}_1$ can also be characterized in terms of truth tables. In what follows, truth tables are always understood as full truth tables with lines for all possible combinations of truth-values of all the sentence letters in the sentence.

THEOREM 2.8.

(i) *A sentence of $\mathcal{L}_1$ is logically true (or a tautology) if and only if there are only T's in the main column of its truth table.*

(ii) *A sentence is a contradiction if and only if there are only F's in the main column of its truth table.*

(iii) *A sentence ϕ and a sentence ψ are logically equivalent if and only if they agree on the truth-values in their main columns.*

One of the main purposes of developing semantics for $\mathcal{L}_1$ was to define the notion of a valid argument in $\mathcal{L}_1$ that would be analogous to Characterization 1.9 of validity for arguments in English.

DEFINITION 2.9. *Let Γ be a set of sentences of $\mathcal{L}_1$ and ϕ a sentence of $\mathcal{L}_1$. The argument with all sentences in Γ as premisses and ϕ as conclusion is valid if and only if there is no $\mathcal{L}_1$-structure in which all sentences in Γ are true and ϕ is false.*

The phrase 'The argument with all sentences in Γ as premisses and ϕ as conclusion is valid' will be abbreviated by '$\Gamma \vDash \phi$'; this is also often read as 'ϕ follows (logically) from Γ' or as 'Γ (logically) implies ϕ' or as 'ϕ is a logical consequence of Γ'. Thus $\Gamma \vDash \phi$ if and only if the following holds for all $\mathcal{L}_1$-structures $\mathcal{A}$:

If $|\psi|_{\mathcal{A}} = \text{T}$ for all $\psi \in \Gamma$, then $|\phi|_{\mathcal{A}} = \text{T}$.

Thus an $\mathcal{L}_1$-argument is not valid iff there is a structure that makes all premises true and the conclusion false:

DEFINITION 2.10. *An $\mathcal{L}_1$-structure is a counterexample to the argument with Γ as the set of premises and ϕ as conclusion if and only if $|\psi|_{\mathcal{A}} = T$ for all $\psi \in \Gamma$ and $|\phi|_{\mathcal{A}} = F$.*

Therefore, an argument in $\mathcal{L}_1$ is valid if and only if it does not have a counterexample.

Following the pattern of Definition 1.10 of consistency for sets of sentences in English I will define consistency for sets of $\mathcal{L}_1$-sentences:

DEFINITION 2.11 (SEMANTIC CONSISTENCY). *A set Γ of $\mathcal{L}_1$-sentences is semantically consistent if and only if there is an $\mathcal{L}_1$-structure $\mathcal{A}$ such that $|\phi|_{\mathcal{A}} = T$ for all sentences ϕ of Γ. Semantic inconsistency is just the opposite of semantic consistency: a set Γ of $\mathcal{L}_1$-sentences is semantically inconsistent if and only if Γ is not consistent.*[4]

After Definition 1.10 I argued that an argument is valid if and only if the set obtained by adding the negation of the conclusion to the premisses is inconsistent. The argument carries over to $\mathcal{L}_1$:

THEOREM 2.12. *If ϕ and all elements of Γ are $\mathcal{L}_1$-sentences, then the following obtains:*

> $\Gamma \vDash \phi$ *if and only if the set containing all sentences in Γ and $\neg\phi$ is semantically inconsistent.*

Thus, for an argument with, say, two premises ϕ and ψ and a conclusion χ, this means that $\phi, \psi \vDash \chi$ if and only if the set $\{\phi, \psi, \neg\chi\}$ is semantically inconsistent. The proof of the theorem is left to the reader.

Logicians usually allow infinite sets of premises, but such infinite sets of premises will not play an important role here. One can actually

---

4 There is an alternative way of defining the consistency of sets of $\mathcal{L}_1$-sentences, which is known as 'syntactic consistency'. Although the definition looks very different, both notions of consistency coincide. Syntactic consistency will be introduced in Definition 7.5.

prove that if a sentence ϕ of $\mathcal{L}_1$ follows from a set Γ of sentences, then ϕ already follows from a finite set of sentences in Γ. This result is known as the Compactness Theorem of propositional logic.

The set Γ of premisses may also be empty. A sentence follows from the empty set of premisses if and only if it is a tautology (that is, iff it is logically true). This is fairly obvious; it is also a special case of Theorem 2.14 below.

If Γ has only finitely many elements, one can use truth tables to check whether $\Gamma \vDash \phi$. I will show how to answer the question whether $\Gamma \vDash \phi$ by means of an example.

EXAMPLE 2.13. $\{P \to \neg Q, Q\} \vDash \neg P$.

Claims like the one above may be abbreviated by dropping the curly brackets around the premisses. So '$\psi_1, \ldots, \psi_n \vDash \phi$', *where* $\psi_1, \ldots, \psi_n$, *and* ϕ *are* $\mathcal{L}_1$-*sentences, is short for* '$\{\psi_1, \ldots, \psi_n\} \vDash \phi$'. So the claim of Example 2.13 may be written $P \to \neg Q, Q \vDash \neg P$.

First I draw a truth table for the premisses and the conclusion in the following way:

P	Q	$P \to \neg Q$	Q	$\neg P$
T	T	T **F** F T	**T**	**F** T
T	F	T **T** T F	**F**	**F** T
F	T	F **T** F T	**T**	**T** F
F	F	F **T** T F	**F**	**T** F

(2.1)

Now I will check whether there is any line in which the entries in the main columns of the premisses all have T's, while the conclusion has an F. In the first line of truth-values the first premiss receives an F, the second a T, and the conclusion an F. The second and fourth lines also have F's for one premiss. The third line has T's for both premisses, but also a T for the conclusion. Thus, there is no line where all premisses receive T's and the conclusion an F. Therefore, the argument is valid, that is, $\neg P$ follows from $\{P \to \neg Q, Q\}$ or, formally, $P \to \neg Q, Q \vDash \neg P$.

For finite sets Γ of premisses, one can reduce the problem of checking whether $\Gamma \vDash \phi$ to the problem of checking whether a single sentence is logically true. To do this one combines all of the premisses, that is, all sentences in Γ, using ∧, and then one puts the resulting conjunction in front of an arrow followed by the conclusion. The resulting sentence is logically true if and only if the argument is valid. This can be expressed more succinctly as follows:

THEOREM 2.14. $\psi_1, \ldots, \psi_n \vDash \phi$ *if and only if* $\psi_1 \wedge \ldots \wedge \psi_n \to \phi$ *is a tautology (that is, iff* $\psi_1 \wedge \ldots \wedge \psi_n \to \phi$ *is logically true).*

I do not give a proof of this theorem here.

I will apply Theorem 2.14 to the example above: First, the two premisses are combined into $(P \to \neg Q) \wedge Q$. It is necessary to reintroduce the brackets around $P \to \neg Q$ because otherwise the result would be an abbreviation for $P \to (\neg Q \wedge Q)$ as ∧ binds more strongly than →. Next, the arrow is put between this conjunction and the conclusion. This yields $((P \to \neg Q) \wedge Q) \to \neg P$. The brackets around the conjunction of the two premisses are not really necessary since ∧ binds more strongly than →, but they might make the sentence easier to read. The truth table for this long sentence looks like this:

P	Q	$((P$	$\to$	$\neg$	$Q)$	$\wedge$	$Q)$	$\to$	$\neg$	P
T	T		T	F	F T	F	T	T	F	T
T	F		T	T	T F	F	F	T	F	T
F	T		F	T	F T	T	T	T	T	F
F	F		F	T	T F	F	F	T	T	F

(2.2)

Thus, the sentence $((P \to \neg Q) \wedge Q) \to \neg P$ is valid, that is, it is a tautology. By Theorem 2.14, it follows that $P \to \neg Q, Q \vDash \neg P$. Of course, we know this already from truth table (2.1).

Drawing truth tables for arguments or sentences with many sentence letters is cumbersome as every new sentence letter doubles the number of lines of the truth table. This is because for any already given line two possibilities must be considered: the new sentence letter can have truth-value T or F. Therefore, a sentence or argument with 1 sentence letter requires only 2 lines, one with 2 different sentence letters requires 4, one with 3 requires 8 lines, and so on. In general, the truth table for a sentence or argument with n different sentence letters will have 2^n lines of truth-values.

When writing down a truth table with all the lines, one should list all cases in a systematic way, so one does not forget a line. In a truth table with 3 sentence letters, for instance, one should write down 4 T's and then 4 F's in the first column. In the second column one writes down 2 T's and 2 F's and then repeats this for those lines with an F in the first column. Finally in the third line one begins with a T in the first line followed by an F in the second and then repeats this. For an example see page 72.

To show that an $\mathcal{L}_1$-sentence is a tautology, one does not need to draw a complete truth table. One only needs to show that there cannot be a line in the truth table that yields an F in the main column. In order to refute the existence of such a line for Example 2.13, the best strategy is to start with the assumption that the value in the main column is F:

$$
\begin{array}{c|c||cccccc}
P & Q & ((P & \to & \neg\, Q) & \wedge & Q) & \to & \neg\, P \\
\hline
 & & & & & & & \mathbf{F} &
\end{array}
$$

A sentence of the form $\phi \to \psi$ has the truth-value F only if ϕ has truth-value T and ψ has truth-value F. Thus, I must have:

$$
\begin{array}{c|c||cccccc}
P & Q & ((P & \to & \neg\, Q) & \wedge & Q) & \to & \neg\, P \\
\hline
 & & & & & & \mathrm{T} & & \mathbf{F}\ \mathrm{F}
\end{array}
$$

I can continue to calculate truth-values 'backwards':

$$
\begin{array}{c|c||cccccc}
P & Q & ((P & \to & \neg\, Q) & \wedge & Q) & \to & \neg\, P \\
\hline
 & & & & \mathrm{T} & & \mathrm{T\,T} & \mathbf{F}\ \mathrm{F}\ \mathrm{T}
\end{array}
$$

I write the calculated truth-values also under the first two occurrences of P and Q:

$$
\begin{array}{c|c||cccccc}
P & Q & ((P & \to & \neg\, Q) & \wedge & Q) & \to & \neg\, P \\
\hline
 & & \mathrm{T\,T\,?\,T} & & \mathrm{T\,T} & & \mathbf{F}\ \mathrm{F}\ \mathrm{T}
\end{array}
$$

But now there is no way to continue. The slot marked with a question mark cannot be filled with a truth-value: there should be an F under the negation symbol ¬, as Q has truth-value T, but there should also be a T, because $(P \to \neg Q)$ and P have T's. It follows that there cannot be a line with an F in the main column. Therefore, in the full truth table with all the lines, all truth-values in the main column are T's. This proves again that $((P \to \neg Q) \wedge Q) \to \neg P$ is a tautology.

Since it is not easy (for an examination marker, for instance) to reconstruct how the truth-values have been calculated, it is useful to record the order in which the values were obtained:

$$
\begin{array}{c|c||ccccccccc}
P & Q & ((P & \to & \neg & Q) & \wedge & Q) & \to & \neg & P \\
\hline
 & & & T_6 & T_3 & ? & T_7 & T_1 & T_4 & \mathbf{F} & F_2 & T_5
\end{array}
$$

Of course I could have written down the truth-values in a different order. For instance, after arriving at F_2, I could have calculated the value in the last column and only then have turned to the part preceding $\to$.

Now I will use the same method to show that $(P \to \neg Q) \to \neg P$ is not a tautology. As before, an F is written in the main column:

$$
\begin{array}{c|c||cc}
P & Q & (P \to \neg Q) & \to & \neg & P \\
\hline
 & & & \mathbf{F}
\end{array}
$$

The following table results from the first backwards-calculation:

$$
\begin{array}{c|c||cccc}
P & Q & (P \to \neg Q) & \to & \neg & P \\
\hline
 & & T & & F & F
\end{array}
$$

Thus, P must receive the truth-value T:

$$
\begin{array}{c|c||cccc}
P & Q & (P \to \neg Q) & \to & \neg & P \\
\hline
 & & T & & F & F & T
\end{array}
$$

Thus one can also write a T under the first occurrence of P:

$$
\begin{array}{c|c||cccc}
P & Q & (P \to \neg Q) & \to & \neg & P \\
\hline
 T & & T & T & & F & F & T
\end{array}
$$

Since $P \to \neg Q$ has the truth-value T and P also has the truth-value T, the sentence $\neg Q$ receives a T, and Q, accordingly, an F. Hence, the line can be completed as follows (I will also insert the obligatory indices):

P	Q	$(P \rightarrow \neg\, Q) \rightarrow \neg\;\; P$
T	F	$T_4\; T_1\; T_5\; F_6$ **F** $\;F_2\; T_3$

At any rate, when one has arrived at a 'possible' line one should calcu-late the truth-values from bottom to top (starting from the truth-values that have been obtained for the sentence letters) to ensure that one has not missed a column that cannot given a unique truth-value. Only once this final check has been carried out, one knows that the line obtained is a possible line in a truth table.

The above backwards-calculations shows that the sentence $(P \rightarrow \neg Q) \rightarrow \neg P$ has truth-value F if P has the truth-value T and Q has the truth-value F.

Technically speaking, if $\mathcal{A}(P) = $ T and $\mathcal{A}(Q) = $ F for a structure $\mathcal{A}$, then $(P \rightarrow \neg Q) \rightarrow \neg P$ is false in $\mathcal{A}$. So, by Definition 2.7(i), $(P \rightarrow \neg Q) \rightarrow \neg P$ is not logically true, that is, it is not a tautology.

Sometimes this method of calculating truth-values backwards re-quires more than one line. This is the case in the following example:

P	Q	$(P \vee \neg\, Q) \leftrightarrow (Q \rightarrow P)$
		F

If a sentence $\phi \leftrightarrow \psi$ is false, there are two possibilities: ϕ could have truth-value T and ψ truth-value F, or, ϕ could have F and ψ could have truth-value T. As such, one has to take these two possibilities into ac-count:

	P	Q	$(P \vee \neg\, Q) \leftrightarrow (Q \rightarrow P)$
1			T F F
2			F F T

I have underlined the truth-values that cannot be uniquely determined, and so more than one possibility (line) needs to be checked.

The rest is routine. The indices in the table below indicate the order in which I arrived at the truth-values. The order in which the values are calculated does not really matter, but the indexing makes it easier to follow the reasoning.

	P	Q	$(P \lor \neg Q) \leftrightarrow (Q \to P)$
1			$F_5\ \underline{T}_1\ ?\ T_6\ \ F\ \ T_3\ \underline{F}_2\ F_4$
2			$F_3\ \underline{F}_1\ F_4\ T_5\ \ F\ \ T_6\ \underline{T}_2\ ?$

Neither of the two lines can be completed. This shows that $(P \lor \neg Q) \leftrightarrow (Q \to P)$ is a tautology.

Of course it can happen that more lines are required and that different cases under consideration have to be split up into further subcases.

The method of backwards-calculation can also be applied in order to check whether an argument is valid or not. To show that an argument is not valid, one has to find a line (that is, a structure) where all of the premisses are true and the conclusion is false. If there is no such line, the argument is valid. Here is an example of how to use the method to determine whether an argument is valid. I have picked an example that forces me to consider several different cases. So, I want to determine whether

$$P \to Q,\ \neg(P_1 \to Q) \lor (P \land P_1) \models (P \leftrightarrow Q) \land P_1.$$

I will start by writing the two premisses and the conclusion in one table. I have to check whether there can be a line in the table where the two premisses come out as true while the conclusion is false. As such, I should start by writing T's in the main columns of the premisses and an F in the main column of the conclusion:

P	Q	P_1	$P \to Q$	$\neg(P_1 \to Q) \lor (P \land P_1)$	$(P \leftrightarrow Q) \land P_1$
			T	T	F

Now I have to make a case distinction: the first sentence could be true because P is false or because Q is true. Similarly, in the case of the other sentences, there is no unique way to continue. Given that I can make a case distinction with respect to any of the three sentences, it is not clear how to proceed. But some ways of proceeding can make the calculations quicker and less complicated. It is useful to avoid as much as possible picking a sentence that will require a new case distinction in the next step. Ultimately though, so long as all possible cases are systematically checked, the order in which one proceeds will not affect the end result.

At this stage in the calculation, a case distinction cannot be avoided, and so I will pick the last sentence: $(P \leftrightarrow Q) \wedge P_1$ can be false either because $P \leftrightarrow Q$ is false or because P_1 is false. I will try to complete the line for the latter case and leave the former for later:

	P	Q	P_1	$P \rightarrow Q$	$\neg(P_1 \rightarrow Q) \vee (P \wedge P_1)$	$(P \leftrightarrow Q) \wedge P_1$
1				**T**	**T**	$\underline{F}_1$ **F**
2				**T**	$F_5\ F_2\ T_4$ **T** ? F_3	**F** $\underline{F}_1$

The second line of the table cannot be completed: the second premiss must be true, but it follows from my assumption that both $\neg(P_1 \rightarrow Q)$ and $P \wedge P_1$ must be false. This means that the rules tell me to write an F in the slot marked by ?, because P_1 is false, but they also tell me to write a T for ?, because the entire sentence $\neg(P_1 \rightarrow Q) \vee (P \wedge P_1)$ is true and $\neg(P_1 \rightarrow Q)$ is already false.

Line 1 is more complicated, because $P \leftrightarrow Q$ can be false for two reasons: first, P can be true while Q is false or, second, P can be false while Q is true. Thus, I need to distinguish the subcases marked 1.1 and 1.2:

	P	Q	P_1	$P \rightarrow Q$	$\neg(P_1 \rightarrow Q) \vee (P \wedge P_1)$	$(P \leftrightarrow Q) \wedge P_1$
1.1				T_5 **T** ?	**T** T_4	$\underline{T}_2\ \underline{F}_1\ \underline{F}_3$ **F**
2				**T**	$F_5\ F_2\ T_4$ **T** ? F_3	**F** $\underline{F}_1$
1.2				**T**	**T**	$\underline{F}_2\ \underline{F}_1\ \underline{T}_3$ **F**

Since P is true and $P \rightarrow Q$ is true, Q has to be true as well. But according to the assumption, Q is false. Therefore, line 1.1 cannot be completed.

Only case 1.2 remains:

	P	Q	P_1	$P \to Q$	$\neg(P_1 \to Q) \vee (P \wedge P_1)$	$(P \leftrightarrow Q) \wedge P_1$
1.1				T_5 **T** ?	**T** T_4	$\underline{T}_2\ \underline{F}_1\ \underline{F}_3$ **F**
2				**T**	$F_5\ F_2\ T_4$ **T** ? F_3	**F** $\underline{F}_1$
1.2				**T**	$F_7\ T_6\ T_5$ **T** F_4 ?	$\underline{F}_2\ \underline{F}_1\ \underline{T}_3$ **F**

Since the second premiss is true and $\neg(P_1 \to Q)$ is false, $P \wedge P_1$ ought to be true. But this cannot be the case, because P is false. So line 1.2 cannot be completed either. Since this exhausts the possible ways of refuting the argument, the following claim has been established:

$$P \to Q,\ \neg(P_1 \to Q) \vee (P \wedge P_1) \vDash (P \leftrightarrow Q) \wedge P_1.$$

The entries in a table where one calculates truth-values 'backwards' should be indexed by numbers that show the order in which the values were obtained. The assumptions in the different cases should be indicated by underlining the respective truth-values. Subcases should be marked as such (in the way I have done this above). A proof without indices for the truth-values will be considered to be incomplete. These conventions merely serve the purpose of making the calculations easier to reconstruct: otherwise the calculations of truth-values can be very difficult to follow.

After having developed semantics for the language $\mathcal{L}_1$, I will now look at alternatives. One might wonder why the connectives $\neg$, $\wedge$, $\vee$, $\to$, and $\leftrightarrow$ have been chosen. These connectives are used in many logic texts, and they more or less correspond to expressions in English. However, there are also other English phrases for connecting sentences. The phrase 'neither ... nor ...' is an example. The sentence

Neither Jones nor Brown is in Barcelona

will be true if and only if Jones is not in Barcelona and Brown is not in Barcelona. In $\mathcal{L}_1$ there is no connective that directly corresponds to 'neither ... nor ...'. If one added a connective for the phrase 'neither ...

nor ...', it would have the following truth table:

ϕ	ψ	$\phi \downarrow \psi$
T	T	F
T	F	F
F	T	F
F	F	T

However, the connective $\downarrow$ for 'neither ... nor ...' is not really needed because one can generate the same truth table using the old connectives of $\mathcal{L}_1$. 'Neither ... nor ...' can be re-expressed in English as 'It is not the case that ..., and it is not the case that ...'. In $\mathcal{L}_1$ one can also define $\downarrow$ in terms of $\neg$ and $\wedge$ in the following way:

ϕ	ψ	$\neg$	ϕ	$\wedge$	$\neg$	ψ
T	T	F		F	F	
T	F	F		F	T	
F	T	T		F	F	
F	F	T		T	T	

Alternatively, one can re-express or define $\phi \downarrow \psi$ as $\neg(\phi \vee \psi)$. Thus, adding $\downarrow$ to the language $\mathcal{L}_1$ would not increase the expressive power of $\mathcal{L}_1$. The connective $\downarrow$ would only allow one to abbreviate some sentences. There are many more truth tables for which $\mathcal{L}_1$ does not have connectives. So far I have looked only at binary connectives (connectives conjoining two sentences) such as $\wedge$, $\vee$, $\rightarrow$, $\leftrightarrow$, and $\downarrow$, but there are also unary connectives (connectives taking one sentence) other than $\neg$; and there are ternary connectives (connectives taking three sentences), and so on. Can all these connectives be expressed with the connectives of $\mathcal{L}_1$, that is, with $\neg$, $\wedge$, $\vee$, $\rightarrow$, and $\leftrightarrow$? The answer is 'yes': all truth tables can be produced with the old connectives of $\mathcal{L}_1$. This fact is called the truth-functional completeness of $\mathcal{L}_1$. In fact, $\neg$ and $\wedge$ together without any further connectives are sufficient for expressing all other connectives. And even $\downarrow$ on its own would do the trick. At any rate, adding more connectives to $\mathcal{L}_1$ than those used here is not really necessary and would not increase the expressive power of $\mathcal{L}_1$. I will not prove these results here.

3 Formalization in Propositional Logic

In the previous chapter I focused on the formal language $\mathcal{L}_1$. The connectives $\wedge$, $\vee$, $\rightarrow$, and $\leftrightarrow$ of $\mathcal{L}_1$ can be used to combine sentences of $\mathcal{L}_1$ to form new compound sentences; the connective $\neg$ can be added in front of a sentence of $\mathcal{L}_1$ to build a new sentence.

English sentences can also be combined and modified with many different connectives to form new sentences. For instance, one can write the word 'and' between two English sentences to obtain a new sentence. 'Or', 'because', 'although', 'but', 'while', 'if', and many others can be used in the same way. An expression that connects sentences can also be more complex: the expression 'due to the fact that' between two English sentences yields a new English sentence. Other expressions, such as 'if ..., then', connect sentences even though they are not written between two sentences.

Other expressions do not combine sentences, but rather modify a sentence, as is the case with 'not', 'as is well known', 'John strongly believes that', and 'regrettably'. 'Not' is special insofar as it often cannot be simply inserted into a sentence, but rather requires the introduction of the auxiliary verb 'to do': the introduction of 'not' into 'Alan went to London' yields 'Alan did not go to London'. In this respect 'not' is more complicated than an adverb such as 'regrettably' or the connective $\neg$ of $\mathcal{L}_1$.

In the previous chapter I defined the notion of a connective; now I will apply it to English as well: *Expressions that can be used to combine or modify English sentences to form a sentence are connectives*. This definition is far from being precise, but an exact definition of the notion of a connective of English is not easy to give because sometimes the connectives are not simply plugged into or written between sentences, because occasionally the sentences themselves have to be modified, for instance, by introducing auxiliary verbs, as the above example of 'not' shows.

3.1 TRUTH-FUNCTIONALITY

The connectives of $\mathcal{L}_1$, that is, $\neg$, $\wedge$, $\vee$, $\rightarrow$, and $\leftrightarrow$, correspond to connectives in English. The semantics of the connectives of $\mathcal{L}_1$ is very simple; it is encompassed in their truth tables. In contrast, many connectives of English function in a much more intricate way.

As an example I will consider the connective 'because'. Imagine that I drop my laptop computer on the street. It's had it: the screen is broken. So my laptop computer does not work. The sentence

> My computer does not work because I dropped my computer

is also true: the laptop would still be functional if I had not dropped it. Moreover, it is true that the computer does not work and it is true that I dropped it. Thus, 'because' connects the two true sentences 'My computer does not work' and 'I dropped my computer' together forming a new true sentence. In this respect it seems similar to 'and'.

In other cases, however, one can use 'because' to connect two true English sentences A and B and end up with a false sentence. After picking up my broken laptop, I consider the following sentence:

> My laptop computer does not work because it is not plugged in.

In the situation I just described, it is true that my computer does not work, and it is true that it is not plugged in as I am standing in the street with my broken laptop. Nevertheless the sentence that my laptop computer does not work because it is not plugged in is false: it would work if I had not dropped it. Even if it were now plugged in, it would not work. It does not work because I dropped it, not because it is not plugged in. So this is a case in which using 'because' to connect two true sentences yields a false sentence.

Nevertheless, the truth of 'A because B' is not completely independent of the truth and falsity of the English sentences A and B. If A or B (or both) are false, then 'A because B' is also false. These dependencies can be summarized in the following truth table for the English connective 'because', where A and B are declarative sentences of English:

A	B	A because B
T	T	?
T	F	F
F	T	F
F	F	F

The question mark indicates that in this case the truth-value of 'A because B' depends not only on the truth-values of the direct subsentences, that is, on the truth-values of the sentences A and B that 'because' connects. This means that when 'because' is used to connect two true sentences, sometimes the resulting sentence is true and sometimes the resulting sentence is false; so the truth-value of the compound sentence is not determined by the truth-values of the sentences connected by 'because'. In this respect 'because' differs from 'and'. If the truth-value of the compound sentence is determined by the truth-value of the connected sentences, as is the case with 'and', then the connective is called 'truth-functional'. Connectives like 'because' are not truth-functional.

CHARACTERIZATION 3.1 (TRUTH-FUNCTIONALITY). *A connective is truth-functional if and only if the truth-value of the compound sentence cannot be changed by replacing a direct subsentence with another sentence having the same truth-value.*

For instance, 'because' is not truth-functional: replacing the true sentence 'I dropped my computer' with the equally true sentence 'the computer is not plugged in' does change the truth-value of the compound sentence

My computer does not work because I dropped my computer

from True to False.

Thus, the definition of truth-functionality of an English connective can be paraphrased in terms of truth tables: a connective is truth-functional if and only if its truth table does not contain any question marks.

'If ... then' is usually translated as the arrow →. Some of its occurrences, however, are definitely not truth-functional. A sentence $\phi \to \psi$ is true if ϕ is false or ψ is true. In the following sentence, 'if ... then' functions differently:

If Giovanni hadn't gone to England, he would not have caught a cold in Cambridge.

Assume that Giovanni really did go to England, but did not catch a cold in Cambridge. In this case one may hesitate to assign a truth-value to the sentence: some people would say that the sentence is neither true nor false; others would say that it is false. At any rate, in that case the sentence is not true. But if the whole sentence is not true, then this is a case in which the first subsentence following 'if' is false, but the whole sentence is also false. But according to the truth table for → a sentence with a false antecedent is true. This means that the arrow → cannot be used to formalize the sentence correctly.

'If'-sentences describing what would have happened under circumstances that are not actual are called 'subjunctives' or 'counterfactuals'. In these sentences 'if' does not function like the arrow → and cannot be translated as the arrow. The proper treatment of counterfactuals is beyond the scope of this book.[1]

Indicative conditionals such as

If Jones gets to the airport an hour late, his plane will wait for him

1 Lewis (1973) is a classic text on counterfactuals.

are often formalized using the arrow →, but it is somewhat questionable whether → really is appropriate.

Assume, for instance, that Jones arrives at the airport early and he easily catches the plane. Suppose also that Jones is not a VIP and so the airline would not have waited for him. Using the arrow for 'if' one can try to translate this sentence as $P \rightarrow Q$ with the following dictionary:

> P: Jones gets to the airport an hour late
> Q: Jones's plane will wait for Jones

If $|P|_\mathcal{A} = F$, that is, if P is false in the structure $\mathcal{A}$, then $P \rightarrow Q$ is true in $\mathcal{A}$, that is, $|P \rightarrow Q|_\mathcal{A} = T$ by Definition 2.6 or by the truth table of → on page 38. According to the assumptions, 'Jones gets to the airport an hour late' is actually false. Thus, if the formalization is correct, the displayed English 'if'-sentence should be true. But it is highly questionable whether it is true: one may hold that 'If Jones gets to the airport an hour late, his plane will wait for him' is simply false, even if Jones gets there on time.

There is an extensive literature on the treatment of 'if'-sentences. The treatment of 'if'-sentences, including counterfactuals, has interesting philosophical implications. I shall not go further into the details of this discussion here. The above example should be sufficient to show that formalizing 'if' by the arrow is problematic even in the case of indicative conditionals. For most purposes, however, the arrow is considered to be close enough to the 'if ... then ...' of English, with the exception of counterfactuals.

The definition of truth-functionality also applies to unary connectives: a unary connective is truth-functional if and only if the truth-value of the sentence with the connective cannot be changed by replacing the direct subsentence with a sentence with the same truth-value.

'It is necessarily the case that A' or 'It is necessary that' is a unary connective that is not truth-functional. If A is a false English sentence, then 'It is necessary that A' is false, but if A is true, 'It is necessary that A' may be either true or false:

It is necessary that all trees are trees.

This sentence is true: 'all trees are trees' is logically true and thus necessary. But, if the true sentence 'All trees are trees' is replaced by the true sentence 'Volker has ten coins in his pocket' then the resulting sentence

It is necessary that Volker has ten coins in his pocket

is not true, as I could easily have had only nine coins in my pocket. In any case, if A is only accidentally true, 'It is necessary that A' will be false. Thus the corresponding truth table looks like this:

A	it is necessary that A
T	?
F	F

Some other connectives – like 'Bill believes that …' – have nothing but question marks in their truth tables. In contrast, 'Bill knows that …' has the same truth table as 'it is necessary that'.[2]

3.2 LOGICAL FORM

In this section and the next I will show how to translate English sentences into $\mathcal{L}_1$ sentences. These translations are carried out in two steps: First the sentence is brought into a standardized form, which is called the '(propositional) logical form'.[3] In the second step the English expressions are replaced by symbols. Obtaining the logical form is the non-trivial part; the step from the logical form to a sentence of the language $\mathcal{L}_1$ of propositional logic is simple and purely mechanical.

2 A more comprehensive account of truth-functionality is given by Sainsbury (2001, chapter 2).

3 In this chapter I will usually drop the specification 'propositional' from 'propositional logical form' since I will not deal with any other kind of logical form for now. There is also a more complex predicate logical form of an English sentence. The predicate logical form will be studied in Chapter 7.

Here I shall sketch a practical procedure for bringing an English sentence into its logical form. The procedure is to be applied to the sentence, reapplied to its sentences from which the main sentence is built up, and then repeated until the subsentences cannot be further analysed by the means of propositional logic.

I have broken down this procedure into five steps. In practice they are all carried out at the same time. The first step is the difficult one: in this step it is checked whether the sentence can be broken down into a truth-functional connective and one or more subsentences, that is, whether the sentence is built up from one or more sentences with a truth-functional connective.

For instance, the sentence

> The car doesn't start because the battery is flat or there is
> no petrol in the tank

is not built up from other sentences with a truth-functional connective: it is built up from the sentence 'The car doesn't start' and the sentence 'The battery is flat or there is no petrol in the tank' with the connective 'because', which is not truth-functional. The connective 'or' is truth-functional, but it only connects 'The battery is flat' and 'There is no petrol in the tank'; so only the subsentence 'The battery is flat or there is no petrol in the tank' is built up from other sentences with the truth-functional connective 'or', but not the entire sentence.

To put it in a different way, one identifies the 'topmost' or 'main' connective and checks whether it is truth-functional. It is permissible to reformulate the sentence slightly to put into a form such that it is built up with a truth-functional connective. The truth-functional connectives should be taken from a fixed list of truth-functional connectives; this restriction will enable one to formalize the connectives as the five connectives of the formal language $\mathcal{L}_1$, respectively. Finally, one reapplies the procedure to the sentence(s) from which the main sentence is built up.

I give now the five steps of the procedure and then show how it works by means of some examples:

1. *Check if the sentence can be reformulated in a natural way as a sentence built up from one or more sentences with a truth-functional connective. If this is not possible, then the sentence should be put in brackets and not analysed any further.*
2. *If the sentence can be reformulated in a natural way as a sentence built up from one or more sentences with a truth-functional connective, do so.*
3. *If that truth-functional connective is not one of the standard connectives in Table 3.1, reformulate the sentence using the standard connectives.*
4. *Enclose the whole sentence in brackets, unless it is a negated sentence, that is, a sentence starting with 'it is not the case that'.*
5. *Apply the procedure, starting back at 1., to the next subsentence(s) (that is, to the sentence(s) without the standard connective from step 3).*

name	standard connective	some other formulations
conjunction	and	but, although
disjunction	or	unless
negation	it is not the case that	not, none, never
arrow	if ... then	provided that ..., ... only if
double arrow	if and only if	exactly if, precisely if

Table 3.1: standard connectives

There is no need to memorize this description of the procedure; the point is to learn how to apply it. Thus instead of describing the procedure in more detail, which would be fairly difficult, I'll illustrate the procedure with several examples:

EXAMPLE 3.2. Rob and Tim will laugh, if the tutor can't pronounce Siobhan's name.

The sentence is built from 'Rob and Tim will laugh' and 'The tutor can't pronounce Siobhan's name' with the connective '..., if ...'. As such, there is no need for the sort of reformulation called for in 2. But '..., if ...' is not a standard connective. So, in accordance with step 3 I will reformulate the sentence with the standard connective 'if ... then ...':

> If the tutor can't pronounce Siobhan's name, then Rob and Tim will laugh.

In step 4 the entire sentence is enclosed by brackets:

> (If the tutor can't pronounce Siobhan's name, then Rob and Tim will laugh)

Step 5 sends me back again to step 1. The two subsentences to which step 1 is applied are:

> The tutor can't pronounce Siobhan's name,

> Rob and Tim will laugh.

The first sentence contains a negation and so I will reformulate it with the standard connective 'it is not the case that ...':

> It is not the case that the tutor can pronounce Siobhan's name.

According to step 4, the sentence does not need to be put in brackets since it starts with 'it is not the case that'.

I still have to apply the procedure to the second sentence. 'Rob and Tim will laugh' is not a sentence built up using a truth-functional connective, but it can be reformulated in accordance with step 2 as a sentence with a truth-functional connective in the following way:

> Rob will laugh and Tim will laugh.

Since '... and ...' is already a standard connective, there is no need for the sort of reformulation described in step 3. After applying step 4 I obtain the following expression:

(Rob will laugh and Tim will laugh)

Thus the whole sentence now reads as follows:

(If it is not the case that the tutor can pronounce Siobhan's name, then (Rob will laugh and Tim will laugh))

Now I have to start again with step 1. The sentence 'the tutor can pronounce Siobhan's name' cannot be reformulated in a natural way as a sentence built up with a truth-functional connective. Thus it is put in brackets according to step 1:

(If it is not the case that (the tutor can pronounce Siobhan's name), then (Rob will laugh and Tim will laugh))

Next, neither 'Rob will laugh' nor 'Tim will laugh' can be reformulated as a sentence built with a truth-functional connective, so they are each put into brackets as required by step 1:

(If it is not the case that (the tutor can pronounce Siobhan's name), then ((Rob will laugh) and (Tim will laugh)))

Now this is the (propositional) logical form of the sentence.

EXAMPLE 3.3. Unless the ignition is turned on and there is petrol in the tank, the engine will not start and I'll not be able to arrive in time.

I can skip steps 1 and 2 because the sentence is already built up with a truth-functional connective, though not by a standard one. Next, I replace 'unless' by the standard connective 'or' in accordance with step 3; then I apply step 4 and enclose the entire sentence in brackets.

(The ignition is turned on and there is petrol in the tank, or the engine will not start and I'll not be able to arrive in time)

Since 'and' is already a standard connective, step 4 is applied twice more.

> ((The ignition is turned on and there is petrol in the tank),
> or (the engine will not start and I'll not be able to arrive in
> time))

Next, I turn to the part of the sentence after 'or'. There are two sentences containing 'not'. According to step 3, they are to be reformulated with the corresponding standard connective.

> ((The ignition is turned on and there is petrol in the tank),
> or (it is not the case that the engine will start and it is not
> the case that I'll be able to arrive in time))

Now step 1 is applied four times:

> (((The ignition is turned on) and (there is petrol in the
> tank)), or (it is not the case that (the engine will start) and
> it is not the case that (I'll be able to arrive in time)))

The process terminates here since the remaining sentences not containing brackets, that is, 'The ignition is turned on' and so on, cannot be further analysed.

3.3 FROM LOGICAL FORM TO FORMAL LANGUAGE

Once the logical form of a sentence has been determined, the translation into the language $\mathcal{L}_1$ of propositional logic is simple.

In order to translate the logical form of an English sentence into $\mathcal{L}_1$ apply the following procedure:

1. *Replace standard connectives by their respective symbols in accordance with the following list:*

standard connective	symbol
and	∧
or	∨
it is not the case that	¬
if ... then ...	→
if and only if	↔

2. *Replace every English sentence by a sentence letter and delete the brackets surrounding the sentence letter.*[4] *Use different sentence letters for distinct (that is, different) sentences and the same sentence letter for multiple occurrences of the same sentence.*
3. *Give a list (the 'dictionary') of all sentence letters in the resulting $\mathcal{L}_1$-sentence together with the respective sentences they have replaced.*

I shall carry out this procedure on Example 3.2. The logical form of that sentence is

(If it is not the case that (the tutor can pronounce Siobhan's name), then ((Rob will laugh) and (Tim will laugh))).

To translate this into $\mathcal{L}_1$ I first replace all standard connectives by the respective symbols, as required by step 1:

(¬ (the tutor can pronounce Siobhan's name) → ((Rob will laugh) ∧ (Tim will laugh))).

According to step 2 the sentences are to be replaced by sentence letters:

$$(\neg P \to (Q \land R)).$$

The formalization is completed by adding the dictionary required in step 3:

P: The tutor can pronounce Siobhan's name
Q: Rob will laugh
R: Tim will laugh

---

4 English sentences usually do not contain any $\mathcal{L}_1$ connectives or brackets. Thus, one will replace with sentence letters exactly those English sentences that could not be further analysed in accordance with step 1 of the procedure on page 58.

This was the logical form of the English sentence from the second example:

(((The ignition is turned on) and (there is petrol in the tank)), or (it is not the case that (the engine will start) and it is not the case that (I'll be able to arrive in time))).

Its formalization is the sentence $((P \land Q) \lor (\neg R \land \neg P_1))$, or, using the bracketing conventions, $(P \land Q) \lor (\neg R \land \neg P_1)$. The dictionary is obvious:

P: The ignition is turned on
Q: There is petrol in the tank
R: The engine will start
P_1:   I'll be able to arrive in time

In both examples, I used the sentence letter P to formalize the first sentence, and Q to formalize the next and so on. This is not obligatory. It would have been equally correct (but awkward) to employ the sentence letter R_{473} instead of P.

3.4 AMBIGUITY

Determining the logical form of an English sentence can be tricky. In some cases there is no unique solution.

Brown is in Barcelona and Jones owns a Ford or Smith owns a Ford.

This sentence is ambiguous: 'and' could have been used to connect the two claims 'Brown is in Barcelona' and 'Jones owns a Ford or Smith owns a Ford'. It could equally well be used to express that there are the following two possibilities: first, Brown is in Barcelona and Jones owns a Ford; second, Smith owns a Ford.

Corresponding to these two possible readings there are at least two possible formalizations of this sentence:

(i) $P \land (Q \lor R)$

(ii) $(P \wedge Q) \vee R$

The dictionary is as follows:

P: Brown is in Barcelona
Q: Jones owns a Ford
R: Smith owns a Ford

The formalizations (i) and (ii) correspond to the two readings of the original English sentence. In a given situation it may be clear which reading is intended, and thus which formalization is preferable. Without further hints, however, one cannot decide between (i) and (ii).

Ambiguities like this are called 'scope ambiguities'. Roughly speaking, the scope of an occurrence of a connective in a sentence is that part of the sentence to which the connective applies. In (i) the connective $\wedge$ applies to the entire sentence, as it connects P and $(Q \vee R)$, while in (ii) the scope of $\wedge$ is only $(P \wedge Q)$.

DEFINITION 3.4 (SCOPE OF A CONNECTIVE IN $\mathcal{L}_1$). *The scope of an occurrence of a connective in a sentence ϕ of $\mathcal{L}_1$ is the occurrence of the smallest subsentence of ϕ that contains this occurrence of the connective.*

By 'subsentence of ϕ' I mean any sentence that is part of ϕ.
In the sentence

$$((P \rightarrow (P \vee Q)) \rightarrow (\neg P \wedge Q))$$

the scope of the second occurrence of the arrow $\rightarrow$ is the entire sentence; the scope of the first occurrence of $\rightarrow$ is the underbraced part of the sentence.

The definition of the scope of an occurrence of a connective refers to the sentence, not to any of its abbreviations. So, the scope of the first occurrence of the arrow in

$$(P \rightarrow P \vee Q) \rightarrow (\neg P \wedge Q)$$

is still the underbraced part, because $P \rightarrow P$ is not a part (subsentence) of the real sentence.

The problem of scope ambiguity highlights a general difference between natural languages such as English and formal languages like $\mathcal{L}_1$: while sentences of English are often ambiguous in their structure, sentences of $\mathcal{L}_1$ are never structurally ambiguous. Thus, there is no chance of translating the ambiguous English sentence into an equally ambiguous sentence of $\mathcal{L}_1$. This will mean that one might have to choose between different possible formalizations of an English sentence.

There are also two possibilities of formalizing the following sentence:

> Brown is in Barcelona and Jones owns a Ford and Smith owns a Ford.

The sentence may be formalized as $(P \wedge Q) \wedge R$ or, alternatively, as $P \wedge (Q \wedge R)$. These are two different sentences of the language $\mathcal{L}_1$. But they are logically equivalent: the two $\mathcal{L}_1$-sentences have the same truth table. Thus, it is does not matter for the purpose of checking validities of arguments and similar properties which formalization is used.

3.5 THE STANDARD CONNECTIVES

The syntax of the connectives of $\mathcal{L}_1$ is very simple: $\neg$ is written in front of a sentence, and the sentence that results from writing $\neg$ in front of a sentence is the negation of that original sentence. The other connectives are written between sentences, and the entire string of expressions is surrounded by brackets. The syntax of the corresponding expressions in English is far more complicated.

The grammar of 'not' is a bit complicated: usually one cannot simply insert 'not' into a sentence to obtain the negation of the sentence. Often the sentence is reformulated with the auxiliary verb 'to do'. 'Bill does not write an essay' is the negation of 'Bill writes an essay'. But there are more ways to express negation: one could also say 'Bill writes no essay'; in this case the negation is expressed by 'no'.

'And' and its counterpart $\wedge$ seem less problematic. In some cases 'and' does not connect complete sentences:

> Liz and Anne are mountaineers.

Here 'and' combines two proper names. The sentence, however, can be seen as an abbreviation of a sentence in which 'and' does connect two sentences:

> Liz is a mountaineer and Anne is a mountaineer.

This sentence can then be formalized with the help of ∧. But the trick does not always work. The sentence

> Liz and Anne are friends

can hardly be rephrased as

> Liz is a friend and Anne is a friend.

Some English sentences can be reformulated in a way that introduces 'and':

> Liz is an Australian mountaineer

can be rephrased as

> Liz is Australian and Liz is a mountaineer.

However, the sentence

> Liz is an avid mountaineer

does not mean the same as

> Liz is avid and that Liz is a mountaineer.

Similarly, the sentence

> Kentaro is a slim sumo-wrestler

cannot be rewritten as

> Kentaro is slim and Kentaro is a sumo-wrestler.

For a slim sumo-wrestler might not be slim at all, but only slim for a sumo-wrestler.

The connective 'but' and similar words are often translated as ∧, although 'but' often indicates a contrast between the two sentences that are combined.

'Or' is fairly straightforward. 'Unless' is in many uses very similar to 'or' and may then be translated by ∨. Often 'either ... or ...' is assumed to be exclusive, that is, 'Either A or B' is taken to be false, if A and B are both true. But there are many cases where 'either ... or ...' is used in the same way as the simple 'or'.

3.6 NATURAL LANGUAGE AND PROPOSITIONAL LOGIC

In the previous sections I have shown how to translate English sentences into sentences of the language $\mathcal{L}_1$ of propositional logic. The concepts of Section 2.4 can now be applied to the sentences that have been obtained as translations.

The sentence of $\mathcal{L}_1$ that is obtained by translating an English sentence into the language of propositional logic is the formalization of that sentence.

I will often speak of 'the formalization' of an English sentence as if there were always exactly one (best) formalization. Of course one always has the choice of different sentence letters, and when one is translating a phrase like the exclusive 'either ... or ...', for which there is no direct equivalent in $\mathcal{L}_1$, one has a choice between different ways of rendering this phrase.

Although these different possibilities show already that there cannot be only a single best formalization, the differences between these formalizations do not really matter, because these differences do not affect the properties of $\mathcal{L}_1$-sentences I am interested in. In particular, one can replace sentence letters in a tautology, that is, in a logically true sentence of $\mathcal{L}_1$ and one will obtain a tautology again as long as the same letter is inserted for all occurrences of a given sentence letter. Thus it does not matter with respect to the property of being logically true which sentence letters are used in a translation. Also, how exactly a connective such as 'either ... or ...' is translated does not matter for the property of being a logical truth, being valid, etc.: whether 'Either it rains or it snows', for instance, is formalized as $(P \vee Q) \wedge \neg (P \wedge Q)$, or as $P \leftrightarrow \neg Q$, or as $\neg P \leftrightarrow Q$ (with the obvious dictionary) does not matter for the validity of an argument in which these formalizations are used, as all these formalizations are logically equivalent.

In some cases, however, there are equally correct formalizations of a sentence that differ in their relevant properties: one of them may be logically true while the other is not, for instance. Ambiguous sentences may have more than one formalization in $\mathcal{L}_1$. In such cases one should be more precise and talk about the formalization of a sentence under a certain reading of that sentence. In what follows I will be less precise and mostly ignore problems of ambiguity.

The notions of Definition 2.7 will now be applied to formalizations of English sentences, and the English sentences will be categorized accordingly.

DEFINITION 3.5.

(i) *An English sentence is a tautology if and only if its formalization in propositional logic is logically true (that is, iff it is a tautology).*

(ii) *An English sentence is a propositional contradiction if and only if its formalization in propositional logic is a contradiction.*

(iii) *A set of English sentences is propositionally consistent if the set of all their formalizations in propositional logic is semantically consistent.*

Instead of saying that a sentence is a tautology one can also describe it as propositionally valid.

The following sentence is a tautology:

Unless Alfred is an eminent logician, it is not the case that both Kurt and Alfred are eminent logicians.

'Unless A, B' can be rephrased as 'if not A, then B' or simply as 'A or B'.

The other steps in the translation are routine, and the following $\mathcal{L}_1$-sentence is obtained as a translation:

$$P \vee \neg(P \wedge Q).$$

The dictionary is as follows:

        P: Alfred is an eminent logician
        Q: Kurt is an eminent logician

The truth table shows that $P \vee \neg(P \wedge Q)$ is a tautology by Theorem 2.8 (i):

P	Q	$P \vee \neg\ (P \wedge Q)$		
T	T	T **T** F	T T T	
T	F	T **T** T	T F F	
F	T	F **T** T	F F T	
F	F	F **T** T	F F F	

Therefore, by Definition 3.5 (i), the sentence 'Unless Alfred is an eminent logician, it is not the case that both Kurt and Alfred are eminent logicians' is a tautology.

In the formal language $\mathcal{L}_1$ of propositional logic, the logically true sentences are exactly the tautologies. In contrast, in English there are logically true sentences that are not tautologies. The sentence 'All logicians are logicians' is logically true but it is not a tautology, because the formalization in propositional logic is a single sentence letter. A single sentence letter never is logically true, that is, it never is a tautology.

Similarly, an English sentence can be contradiction without being a propositional contradiction: The sentence 'There is an oak that is not an oak' is an example.

A set of sentences may be propositionally consistent without being consistent. The inconsistent set containing the three sentences 'All birds can fly', 'Tweety is a bird', 'Tweety can't fly', for instance, is propositionally consistent.

I turn now to the formalization of entire arguments. The formalization of an argument in English is that argument in $\mathcal{L}_1$ that has as its premisses all the formalizations of the premisses of the English argument, and has as its conclusion the formalization of the English conclusion.

DEFINITION 3.6. *An argument in English is propositionally valid if and only if its formalization in $\mathcal{L}_1$ is valid.*

Every propositionally valid argument is also valid, but not every valid argument is propositionally valid (for an example see the argument about Zeno on page 18).

Definition 3.6 is a more formal elaboration of the notion of propositional validity mentioned on page 22. Using the methods developed one can check arguments in English for their propositional validity.

I will consider some examples.

Jones owns a Ford or Brown is in Barcelona. If Brown is in Barcelona, Smith is in Barcelona too. But Smith isn't in Barcelona. Therefore, Jones owns a Ford.

The premisses of this argument are translated as the following sentences:

$$P \vee Q$$
$$Q \rightarrow R$$
$$\neg R$$

The conclusion is then formalized as the sentence P. The sentence letters stand for the following English sentences:

P: Jones owns a Ford
Q: Brown is in Barcelona
R: Smith is in Barcelona

By Definition 3.6 the English argument is propositionally valid if and only if $P \vee Q, Q \rightarrow R, \neg R \vDash P$. The claim that $P \vee Q, Q \rightarrow R, \neg R \vDash P$ can be established, according to Theorem 2.14, by showing that the sentence

$$(P \vee Q) \wedge (Q \rightarrow R) \wedge \neg R \rightarrow P$$

is a tautology:

P	Q	R	((P ∨ Q) ∧ (Q → R)) ∧ ¬ R → P
T	T	T	T T T T T T T F F T T T
T	T	F	T T T F T F F F T F T T
T	F	T	T T F T F T T F F T T T
T	F	F	T T F T F T F T T F T T
F	T	T	F T T T T T T F F T T F
F	T	F	F T T F T F F F T F T F
F	F	T	F F F F F T T F F T T F
F	F	F	F F F F F T F F T F T F

Thus the English argument is propositionally valid.

The following argument might look puzzling and too optimistic with respect to my finances:

> Jones has ten coins in his pocket; and it is not the case that Jones has ten coins in his pocket. Therefore there is £ 100 000 in my bank account.

The premiss can be formalized as $P \wedge \neg P$, and the conclusion as Q, with the obvious dictionary:

P: Jones has ten coins in his pocket
Q: There is £ 100 000 in my bank account

By the truth-table method one can easily establish $P \wedge \neg P \vDash Q$ (see Example 6.9). Therefore the argument is propositionally valid.

The argument looks so puzzling because there is no 'connection' between the premiss and the conclusion: the premiss does not seem to say anything about my bank account. But Characterization 1.9 of a valid argument does not say that the premisses of a valid argument need to be relevant in this way to the conclusion. In this case, the premiss of the argument is a (propositional) contradiction; thus there is no interpretation that would make the premiss true (and the conclusion false); and, therefore, the argument is propositionally valid. This principle, that any argument with a contradiction as premiss is called 'ex falso quodlibet', which is Latin for 'From something false everything (follows)'.

Blocking this kind of argument might seem desirable, but it is not a simple task since abandoning the ex falso quodlibet principle will require abandoning rules that are often applied in reasoning. Only such simple rules are applied in the following argumentation, which starts from 'Jones has ten coins in his pocket' and 'it is not the case that Jones has ten coins in his pocket', and arrives at the conclusion that there is £ 100 000 in my bank account.

> Jones has ten coins in his pocket. So Jones has ten coins in his pocket or there is £ 100 000 in my bank account. But Jones does not have ten coins in his pocket. Therefore there is £ 100 000 in my bank account.

The reasoning may sound odd, but it is hard to tell where things go wrong. If a claim '*A*' is true, surely the weaker claim '*A* or *B*' must be true as well. And from an alternative '*A* or *B*' and the negation 'not-*A*' of the first alternative, one usually concludes '*B*'. If these steps may be used to establish the validity of an argument, then the above argument is valid. Blocking the ex falso quodlibet principle would involve the rejection of one of those steps.

Usually when one hits upon a contradiction, one does not carry on reasoning but rather starts to doubt the premisses. The ex falso quodlibet principle shows that it is pointless to reason on the basis of contradictory premisses, because from such premisses everything follows.

4 The Syntax of Predicate Logic

Many arguments in English are valid without being propositionally valid. That is, these arguments are valid but when they are translated into the language $\mathcal{L}_1$ of propositional logic the resulting argument in $\mathcal{L}_1$ is not valid. An example of a valid argument that is not propositionally valid is the example from page 18:

> Zeno is a tortoise. All tortoises are toothless. Therefore Zeno is toothless.

The argument is not propositionally valid because each of the premisses and the conclusion have to be translated into different sentence letters. This means that in the language of propositional logic the two premisses and the conclusion will be formalized as three sentence letters, for instance, as P and Q, and R. It is certainly not the case that $P, Q \vDash R$. The English argument, however, served as an example of a valid argument in Section 1.5. In order to capture the validity of arguments like this one about Zeno, a formal language more powerful and more sophisticated than the language $\mathcal{L}_1$ of propositional logic is required.

4.1 PREDICATES AND QUANTIFICATION

In this section I shall motivate and introduce the basic elements of the syntax of the language $\mathcal{L}_2$ of predicate logic; the precise definition of a sentence of $\mathcal{L}_2$ will be given in Section 4.2.

For its analysis in predicate logic, a simple sentence like 'Tom loves Mary' must be broken down into its constituents: the sentence contains two designators, 'Tom' and 'Mary', that is, two expressions intended to denote a single object. The expression 'loves' is a 'predicate expression' or 'predicate', for short: it connects the two designators and expresses that a certain relation obtains between Tom and Mary.[1] The predicate 'loves' can take two designators. I indicate the slots where the singular terms can be put by dots: Replacing the two strings of dots in the predicate expression '... loves ...' by designators, respectively, yields a declarative English sentence.

Here are further examples of other sentences built from predicate expressions and designators:

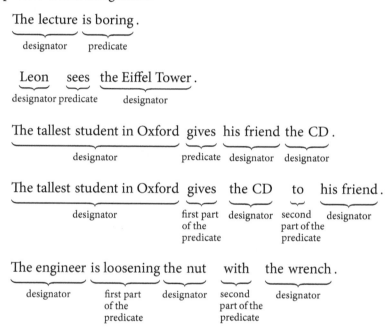

The predicates can be simple and consist in just one word, as is '... sees ...' in the second sentence and '... gives ... ...' in the third; or they can be formed from two or more words, as is '... is boring' in the first sentence, '... gives ... to ...' in the fourth, and '... is loosening ... with ...' in the last.

---

1 The terminology in logic differs here from traditional grammar, where 'loves Mary' would be the predicate.

In predicate logic predicate expressions are translated into predicate letters. These predicates have an upper index that corresponds to the number of designators the corresponding English predicate expression can take. For instance, '... is boring', which can take one designator, is translated into a predicate letter with upper index 1: P^1, for instance, is such a predicate letter. The predicate '... sees ...' can be translated as Q^2 since it can take two designators, and '... gives ... ...' can be translated as R^3 because it can take three designators. The upper index (1, 2, 3 here) is called the predicate letter's 'arity-index'. A predicate letter with upper index n is called an 'n-place predicate letter'. 1-place predicate letters are also called 'unary', 2-place 'binary', and 3-place 'ternary'. So, the predicate expression '... is loosening ... with ...', for instance, is translated into a ternary predicate letter.

It is not hard to find English sentences that require 4- or 5-place predicate letters for their formalization. Thus, I will include predicate letters with arity-indices for any n in the language $\mathcal{L}_2$ of predicate logic to make sure that there is always a sufficient stock of predicate letters available for the various English predicates.

I will also include 0-place predicate letters in the language $\mathcal{L}_2$. They are useful for formalizing English sentences like 'It is raining'. It just seems to be a quirk of the English language that the pronoun 'it' in this sentence is required; 'it' does not serve the same purpose as the designators in the sentences I have considered so far; other languages such as Italian have dispensed with the pronoun in the corresponding sentence. Thus, I will formalize the sentence 'It is raining' and similar sentences as 0-place predicate letters. This provides the reason for including 0-place predicate letters in the language $\mathcal{L}_2$.

Now that I have dealt with predicates, I will turn to the formalization of designators. In the easiest cases the designators are proper names like 'Tom' or 'the Eiffel Tower'; other types of designators will be discussed later. Corresponding to the proper names of English, the language $\mathcal{L}_2$ of predicate logic features constants, namely a, b, c, a_1, b_1, c_1, and so on.

The example sentence 'Tom loves Mary' at the beginning of the section can now be translated into the language $\mathcal{L}_2$ as P^2ab. In such sentences, the predicate letter is always put at the beginning of the sentence. The predicate letter and the two constants are translated as follows:

P^2: ... loves ...

  a: Tom

  b: Mary

The order of the constants in P^2ab is crucial: P^2ba is a formalization of 'Mary loves Tom', which says something different from what 'Tom loves Mary' says.

In the dictionary, the entry for 'loves' contains two strings of dots. They stand for the places that are taken in the sentence by the designators 'Tom' and 'Mary'. In the corresponding formal sentence P^2ab the first place of the binary predicate letter P^2 is taken by a, and the second place is taken by b. Now the first string of dots in '... loves ...' corresponds to the first place of P^2 and the second string of dots corresponds to the second place of P^2. In order to emphasize this correlation, one can attach subscripts to the dots:

P^2: ... $_1$ loves ... $_2$

This is tantamount to the translation for P^2 given above.

If there are subscripts in the dictionary, the string of dots marked 1 always corresponds to the first place of the predicate letter, the string marked 2 corresponds to the second place of the predicate letter, and so on. The number of strings of dots must always correspond to the arity-index of the predicate letter.

Therefore, if I had used

P^2: ... $_2$ loves ... $_1$

as the entry for P^2, while keeping the entries for a and b unchanged, the proper translation of 'Tom loves Mary' would be P^2ba.

As my next example I consider a sentence with a slightly more complicated predicate: The sentence

Ebenezer is a scrooge

can be translated into $\mathcal{L}_2$ as the sentence R^1c, with the following translation of the predicate letter and the constant:

R^1:   ... is a scrooge
  c: Ebenezer

The noun 'scrooge' is not translated separately but forms part of the predicate '... is a scrooge', which is translated as the predicate letter R^1. Typically, phrases of the form 'is a ...' are translated as predicate letters. One way to see why '... is a scrooge' can be translated as a simple predicate letter only, is to observe that instead of 'is a scrooge' one could say 'is stingy', which obviously can be translated as a unary predicate letter.

In the language $\mathcal{L}_2$ an n-place predicate letter followed by n constants yields a sentence. Hence, P^2ab, that is, a binary predicate letter followed by two constants, and R^1c, that is, a unary predicate letter followed by one constant, are sentences of $\mathcal{L}_2$. 0-place predicate letters form a sentence without any further symbol: each 0-place predicate letter is already a sentence. Thus, they behave in the same way as the sentence letters of the language $\mathcal{L}_1$ of propositional logic. In fact, I will identify the 0-place predicate letters with sentence letters; sentence letters are, therefore, merely a certain sort of predicate letters.

One can build sentences of the language $\mathcal{L}_2$ using connectives in the same way as in the language $\mathcal{L}_1$ of propositional logic. For instance, $(P^2ab \wedge R^1c)$ is the translation of the following sentence of $\mathcal{L}_2$:

Tom loves Mary and Ebenezer is a scrooge.

The dictionary is the same as above:

  P^2:   ... loves ...
   a: Tom
   b: Mary
  R^1:   ... is a scrooge
   c: Ebenezer

The techniques for translation into propositional logic carry over to predicate logic (see page 67): 'Liz is an Australian mountaineer' can be rephrased as 'Liz is Australian and Liz is a mountaineer'. The caveats explained there also apply to predicate logic.

With the techniques developed so far, certain occurrences of personal pronouns can be readily translated.

Caesar came, he saw, he conquered.

This can be paraphrased as the following sentence:

Caesar came and Caesar saw and Caesar conquered.

The pronouns (or rather their occurrences) in this example are known as 'lazy' pronouns.[2] Using 'he' here saves one the effort of repeating the name 'Caesar'. Lazy pronouns can easily be eliminated by repeating the name (or whatever they refer back to), and thus their formalizations do not pose any special problems.

There are other uses of pronouns that cannot easily be dispensed with.

If a politician speaks the truth, he won't be elected.

In this sentence the pronoun 'he' cannot be replaced by 'a politician'. The sentence

If a politician speaks the truth, a politician won't be elected

has a different meaning; it says that some politician will not be elected if some politician (not necessarily the same one) speaks the truth. In fact, the original sentence is equivalent to

All politicians speaking the truth are not elected.

2 This terminology comes from Geach (1962).

In the original sentence 'If a politician speaks the truth, he won't be elected' the pronoun is used to express a generalization. Uses of pronouns for the purpose of generalization (and some similar purposes) are called 'quantificational' uses. Quantification can be expressed in many different ways in English. Sometimes pronouns are used, and sometimes quantification can be expressed without pronouns, as is the case with 'All politicians speaking the truth are not elected'.

At any rate, the translation of quantificational uses of pronouns requires additional resources in $\mathcal{L}_2$ beyond the ones I have mentioned so far. Personal pronouns in English come in different genders ('he', 'she', 'it'), in different cases ('he', 'him', and so on). These different forms help to disambiguate sentences. Here is a somewhat tricky case:

> If a visitor wants to borrow a book from the library, she is required to complete the form for it, which must then be submitted to a librarian, who can grant her permission to check it out, if it looks satisfactory to him.

In order to make the reference of the various occurrences of the personal pronouns clearer, one can attach indices to them:

> If a visitor$_1$ wants to borrow a book$_2$ from the library, she$_1$ is required to complete the form$_3$ for it$_2$, which$_3$ must then be submitted to a librarian$_4$, who can grant her$_1$ permission to check it$_2$ out, if it$_3$ looks satisfactory to him$_4$.

It is natural to assume that the first and second occurrences of 'it' refer back to 'book', while the third occurrence refers back to 'the form'. This assumption is made explicit by using subscripts. Natural languages offer other resources for disambiguation, but indexing is a straightforward method. Since the help of gender etc. is no longer required, when the reference is made clear by indexing, one can dispense with English pronouns and replace them with what logicians call variables:

> If a visitor x_1 wants to borrow a book x_2 from the library, x_1 is required to complete the form x_3 for x_2, which$_3$ must

then be submitted to a librarian x_4, who can grant x_1 permission to check x_2 out, if x_3 looks satisfactory to x_4.

In the sentence variables refer back to such phrases as 'a visitor' and 'some book'. One could introduce expressions corresponding to these phrases into the formal language. Logicians have found a method to simplify the language further and to manage with just one additional expression: The purpose of expressions such as 'a visitor' is to restrict the focus to visitors; the above sentence makes a general claim about visitors. But one can replace this with a general claim about all things (whether they are persons, animals, or inanimate objects). Instead of saying

> Every visitor is a classicist,

one can say

> If something is a visitor, then it is a classicist

or

> For everything$_1$: if it$_1$ is a visitor, then it$_1$ is a classicist.

By substituting variables one obtains:

> For all x_1, if x_1 is a visitor, then x_1 is a classicist.

The last formulation is basically the analysis of typical quantified statements. 'For all' is translated as the symbol $\forall$ (a rotated 'A' reminding one of 'all').

'Is a visitor' is a predicate that is translated as P^1, while 'is a classicist' is translated as Q^1. So 'x_1 is a visitor' is translated as P^1x_1, and 'x_1 is a classicist' becomes Q^1x_1. 'If…, then…' becomes the arrow, so 'if x_1 is a visitor, then x_1 is a classicist' becomes $(P^1x_1 \rightarrow Q^1x_1)$. Thus the sentence 'Every visitor is a classicist' translates into the following $\mathcal{L}_2$-sentence:

$$\forall x_1(P^1x_1 \rightarrow Q^1x_1)$$

In addition to $\forall$ logicians also use the symbol $\exists$. In the following sentence an existence claim is made:

At least one visitor is a classicist.

If this is rewritten with variables, then the following expression is obtained:

For at least one x_1, x_1 is a visitor and x_1 is a classicist.

This is then formalized as $\exists x_1 (P^1 x_1 \wedge Q^1 x_1)$.

Later, formalization in predicate logic will be discussed in more detail, but I have now motivated all elements of the syntax of predicate logic that will be introduced in the formal definition of a sentence of $\mathcal{L}_2$.

4.2 THE SENTENCES OF $\mathcal{L}_2$

In this section the syntax of $\mathcal{L}_2$ is introduced in a formally precise way. First I turn to predicate letters.

The language $\mathcal{L}_2$ of predicate logic contains 0-place predicate letters. For simplicity, they do not have an arity-index, that is, an upper index; they are the sentence letters P, Q, R, P_1, Q_1, and so on. $\mathcal{L}_2$ also contains predicate letters with arbitrary arity-index 1, 2, 3, and so on. Having only one binary, that is, 2-place, predicate letter will not suffice. In order to formalize a sentence containing the predicate expressions '... hates ...' and '... loves ...', one will need two distinct binary predicate letters; and of course one might also need a third and even more binary predicate letters. In order to make sure that there is always a sufficient stock of binary predicate letters, I include infinitely many binary predicate letters in $\mathcal{L}_2$, namely the expressions P^2, Q^2, R^2, P_1^2, Q_1^2, R_1^2, P_2^2, and so on. This applies not only to binary predicate letters but also to predicate letters with other arity-indices. Thus, the general definition of predicate letters looks like this:

DEFINITION 4.1 (PREDICATE LETTERS). *All expressions of the form P_n^k, Q_n^k, or R_n^k are predicate letters, where k is either missing (no symbol) or a numeral '1', '2', '3', ... and similarly, n is either missing (no symbol) or a numeral '1', '2', '3', ...*

So the letter P with or without numerals '1', '2', and so on as upper and/or lower indices is a predicate letter, and similarly for Q and R. The sentence letters P, Q, R, P_1, Q_1, … are also predicate letters, according to this definition. Furthermore, P^1, Q^1, R^1, P_1^1, Q_1^1, R_1^1, P_2^1, Q_2^1, R_2^1, …, P_1^2, Q_1^2, R_1^2, P_2^2, Q_2^2, R_2^2, and so on, are predicate letters. This definition ensures that $\mathcal{L}_2$ contains infinitely many n-place predicate letters for any n. Using only predicate letters with P, but not Q or R, would suffice, but having a choice between letters enables me to generate more readable formulae.

0-place predicate letters (sentence letters) have arity 0; 1-place predicate letters have arity 1, and so on:

DEFINITION 4.2. *The value of the upper index of a predicate letter is called its arity. If a predicate letter does not have an upper index its arity is 0.*

The predicate letter P_4^3, for example, has arity 3.

The language $\mathcal{L}_2$ contains constants, which will be used to translate English proper names and some similar expressions.

DEFINITION 4.3 (CONSTANTS). *a, b, c, a_1, b_1, c_1, a_2, b_2, c_2, a_3, …are constants.*

Moreover, $\mathcal{L}_2$ contains infinitely many variables.

DEFINITION 4.4 (VARIABLES). *x, y, z, x_1, y_1, z_1, x_2, …are variables.*

Now the notion of an atomic $\mathcal{L}_2$-formula can be defined:

DEFINITION 4.5 (ATOMIC FORMULAE OF $\mathcal{L}_2$). *If Z is a predicate letter of arity n and each of t_1, …, t_n is a variable or a constant, then $Zt_1 \ldots t_n$ is an atomic formula of $\mathcal{L}_2$.*

In this definition, the upper case letter Z serves as a metavariable for predicate letters, that is, for P, R_{45}^2, Q^1, and the like. According to this definition, Q^1x, P^2cy, $P_5^3x_{31}c_4y$, and R^2xx are examples of atomic formulae. Definition 4.5 allows for the case in which $n = 0$. This means that all sentence letters, that is, P, Q, R, P_1, and so on, are also atomic formulae.

DEFINITION 4.6. *A quantifier is an expression $\forall v$ or $\exists v$ where v is a variable.*

Thus, $\forall x_{348}$ and $\exists z$ are quantifiers.[3]

DEFINITION 4.7 (FORMULAE OF $\mathcal{L}_2$).

  (i) *All atomic formulae of $\mathcal{L}_2$ are formulae of $\mathcal{L}_2$.*
 (ii) *If ϕ and ψ are formulae of $\mathcal{L}_2$, then $\neg\phi$, $(\phi \wedge \psi)$, $(\phi \vee \psi)$, $(\phi \rightarrow \psi)$, and $(\phi \leftrightarrow \psi)$ are formulae of $\mathcal{L}_2$.*
(iii) *If v is a variable and ϕ is a formula, then $\forall v\, \phi$ and $\exists v\, \phi$ are formulae of $\mathcal{L}_2$.*

Examples of formulae of the language $\mathcal{L}_2$ of predicate logic are:

$$\forall x\, (P^2 xa \rightarrow Q^1 x)$$
$$\forall z_{77}\, \neg \exists y_3\, \exists z_{45} (P^2 xy \rightarrow \exists x_2 (R_3^4 z_{77} c_3 x z_{77} \wedge Q))$$
$$(\exists x\, P^1 x \leftrightarrow \neg \exists y\, \exists y\, Q^2 yy)$$
$$\forall x\, \exists z\, R^2 az$$

There is no point in trying to find analogues in English for these formulae. They are only supposed to demonstrate how formulae can be formed in $\mathcal{L}_2$.

In order to show that a given expression is a formula of $\mathcal{L}_2$, one can build up the formula step by step according to the rules laid down in Definition 4.7. As an example I will show that the last formula, $(\exists x P^1 x \leftrightarrow \neg \exists y \exists y Q^2 yy)$, is a formula of $\mathcal{L}_2$:

  1. P^1 is a predicate letter by Definition 4.1 with arity 1 by Definition 4.2, and x is a variable by Definition 4.4.
  2. Therefore, by Definition 4.5, $P^1 x$ is an atomic formula and therefore a formula by Definition 4.7(i).
  3. $\exists x\, P^1 x$ is thus a formula of $\mathcal{L}_2$ by Definition 4.7(iii).
  4. Similarly, $Q^2 yy$ is an atomic formula (I will not go through the tedious reasoning of 1. and 2. again).

---

3 There are alternative symbols for $\forall$ and $\exists$, which will not be used here: $\bigwedge v$, Πv, and (v) are sometimes used instead of $\forall v$, and $\bigvee v$ and Σv instead of $\exists v$.

5. $\exists y\, Q^2 yy$ is a formula of $\mathcal{L}_2$ by 4.7(iii).
6. $\exists y\, \exists y\, Q^2 yy$ is a formula of $\mathcal{L}_2$ by 4.7(iii).
7. $\neg \exists y\, \exists y\, Q^2 yy$ is a formula of $\mathcal{L}_2$ by 4.7(ii).
8. $(\exists x\, P^1 x \leftrightarrow \neg \exists y\, \exists y\, Q^2 yy)$ is a formula of $\mathcal{L}_2$ by 4.7(ii). This follows from the previous item and 3.

Usually one will be able to see without a proof whether an expression that is not too long is a formula or not, and so it will not be necessary to go through all of these steps. The above proof of the claim that $(\exists x\, P^1 x \leftrightarrow \neg \exists y\, \exists y\, Q^2 yy)$ is a formula only shows how exactly the definition of $\mathcal{L}_2$-formulae works.

4.3 FREE AND BOUND OCCURRENCES OF VARIABLES

In the formula $\forall x\, (P^1 x \to Q^1 x)$ the last two occurrences of x refer back to or depend on the quantifier $\forall x$. In the formula $P^1 x \to Q^1 x$, by contrast, there is no quantifier to which they can refer back; they occur freely, as logicians say. In the next definition this notion of a free occurrence of a variable is made precise.

DEFINITION 4.8.

(i) *All occurrences of variables in atomic formulae are free.*
(ii) *The occurrences of a variable that are free in ϕ and ψ are also free in $\neg\phi$, $(\phi \wedge \psi)$, $(\phi \vee \psi)$, $(\phi \to \psi)$, and $(\phi \leftrightarrow \psi)$.*
(iii) *In a formula $\forall v\, \phi$ or $\exists v\, \phi$ no occurrence of the variable v is free; all occurrences of variables other than v that are free in ϕ are also free in $\forall v\, \phi$ and $\exists v\, \phi$.*

An occurrence of a variable is bound in a formula if and only if it is not free.

Less formally speaking, occurrences of variables are free as long as they are not 'caught' by a quantifier. For instance, in the atomic formulae $R^2 xx$ or $P^1 x$ all occurrences of x are free according to clause (i) of the definition, and so, according to clause (ii), all occurrences of x

are free in $(R^2xx \lor \neg P^1x)$ and in $\neg(P^1x \leftrightarrow R^2aa)$. Similarly, all occurrences of x_1 are free in $(P^1x_1 \to Q^1x_1)$, but, according to clause (iii) of Definition 4.8, all occurrences of x_1 are bound in $\forall x_1\,(P^1x_1 \to Q^1x_1)$. In $\forall y\,(P^1x_1 \to Q^1x_1)$ all occurrences of the variable x_1 are free because y is a variable different from x_1.

In $\neg(Q^1z \land \exists z\,R^2zz)$ the first occurrence of the variable z is free, while the remaining occurrences are bound. In $\forall x\,(R^2xy \to R^2xa) \leftrightarrow R^2ax$ all but the last occurrence of x are bound.

DEFINITION 4.9. *A variable occurs freely in a formula if and only if there is at least one free occurrence of the variable in the formula.*

As pointed out on page 81, $\forall x_1\,(P^1x_1 \to Q^1x_1)$ is the formalization of the sentence 'Every visitor is a classicist' with the following logical form:

For everything$_1$: if it$_1$ is a visitor, then it$_1$ is a classicist.

The sentence can be true or false depending on the circumstances. The formula $(P^1x_1 \to Q^1x_1)$ corresponds to

(F)　if it$_1$ is a visitor, then it$_1$ is a classicist.

On its own (F) is not a sentence that is true or false: There is no quantifying phrase like 'for everything$_1$' the pronoun 'it$_1$' can refer back to; also, 'it$_1$' is not a lazy pronoun referring back to a certain designator. Thus, (F) does not have a truth-value. One can only assign a truth-value to (F), if one makes an arbitrary choice and takes 'it$_1$' to stand for a particular thing. But without such an arbitrary choice (F) cannot be assigned a truth-value.

The formulae of $\mathcal{L}_2$ behave similarly: only formulae without free occurrences of variables are sentences; and only sentences will be assigned truth-values by $\mathcal{L}_2$-structures, which will be introduced in the following chapter. Also, sentences but not formulae with free occurrences of variables will be used as premisses and conclusions in arguments.

DEFINITION 4.10 (SENTENCE OF $\mathcal{L}_2$). *A formula of $\mathcal{L}_2$ is a sentence of $\mathcal{L}_2$ if and only if no variable occurs freely in the formula.*

Again informally speaking, in a sentence of $\mathcal{L}_2$ all occurrences of variables are 'caught' by some quantifier. The following are examples of $\mathcal{L}_2$-sentences:

$$\forall x \, (P^1 x \rightarrow (Q^2_{29} x a \vee \exists x \, R^3 x a x))$$
$$(P^2 ab \wedge \exists y (P^2 by \wedge \forall x \, \neg P^2 xy))$$

4.4 NOTATIONAL CONVENTIONS

In Section 2.3 I introduced some conventions for dropping brackets from sentence of $\mathcal{L}_1$. These rules did not form part of the official syntax of $\mathcal{L}_1$; they merely allowed one to abbreviate sentences.

In this section I will specify some rules for abbreviating formulae of $\mathcal{L}_2$. Again, they do not form part of the official syntax. Applying the rules does not yield $\mathcal{L}_2$-sentences but rather only abbreviations of $\mathcal{L}_2$-sentences. Like the rules for dropping brackets in $\mathcal{L}_1$, the conventions do not have to be applied: one can always write down the full formula instead of the abbreviated form.

The Bracketing Conventions 1–3 apply also to formulae of $\mathcal{L}_2$. The quantifiers have to be taken into account: In the sentence $\exists x (P^1 x \wedge Q^1 x)$ the brackets are not outer brackets, so they cannot be dropped. The expression $\exists x \, P^1 x \wedge Q^1 x$ is an abbreviation of the formula $(\exists x \, P^1 x \wedge Q^1 x)$, which is not a sentence, because the second occurrence of x is free.

As a further example I will consider the following $\mathcal{L}_2$-sentence:

$$\forall x \, ((P^1 x \wedge R^2_5 x a) \rightarrow \exists y_2 ((R^2_5 x y_2 \wedge Q^1 x) \wedge P^1 y_2)) \qquad (4.1)$$

This sentence may be abbreviated in the following ways:

$$\forall x \, (P^1 x \wedge R^2_5 x a \rightarrow \exists y_2 ((R^2_5 x y_2 \wedge Q^1 x) \wedge P^1 y_2))$$
$$\forall x \, ((P^1 x \wedge R^2_5 x a) \rightarrow \exists y_2 (R^2_5 x y_2 \wedge Q^1 x \wedge P^1 y_2))$$
$$\forall x \, (P^1 x \wedge R^2_5 x a \rightarrow \exists y_2 (R^2_5 x y_2 \wedge Q^1 x \wedge P^1 y_2))$$

In the first line, only Bracketing Convention 3 is applied, in the second Bracketing Convention 2, and in the third both conventions are applied. There are no further ways of saving brackets.

Very often the upper index of predicate letters, that is, their arity-index, is also omitted. This is due to the fact that there is only one way to add these upper indices to the predicate letters of an expression that is supposed to abbreviate a formula. Therefore, sentence (4.1) also has

$$\forall x \, ((Px \wedge R_5 x a) \rightarrow \exists y_2 ((R_5 x y_2 \wedge Qx) \wedge P y_2))$$

as an abbreviation. So, combined with the rules for dropping brackets, the most economical form of (4.1) is the following abbreviation:

$$\forall x \, (Px \wedge R_5 x a \rightarrow \exists y_2 (R_5 x y_2 \wedge Qx \wedge P y_2))$$

Thus, when the arity-index is missing, this does not necessarily mean that the predicate letter is a sentence letter: it could be an abbreviation of another predicate letter from which the arity-index has been omitted.

Therefore abbreviations of formulae that have been obtained by omitting arity-indices can be misleading: one might think that the expression $\forall x \, \forall y \, (Px \leftrightarrow Pxy)$ abbreviates an $\mathcal{L}_2$-sentence that contains the same predicate letter twice. Inserting the missing indices shows that the sentence contains two different predicate letters, P^1 and P^2:

$$\forall x \, \forall y \, (P^1 x \leftrightarrow P^2 xy)$$

Therefore, there is only one occurrence of P^1 in the formula and only one occurrence of P^2. The abbreviation $\forall x \, \forall y \, (Px \leftrightarrow Pxy)$ is correct according to the above conventions, but in such cases it may be helpful to retain the arity-indices.

4.5 FORMALIZATION

The basic strategy for obtaining the logical form of an English sentence in predicate logic is the same as in propositional logic (cf. Sections

3.2 and 3.3): a given sentence is analysed from top to bottom. That is, one starts with the entire sentence and works one's way deeper and deeper into the sentence. In contrast to propositional logic, one does not have to stop at quantified sentences; one can analyse them in the way outlined in Section 4.1. In particular, the logical form of universal sentences is obtained in the way sketched on page 81.

Rather than going over the general rules again, I will show how the method works by way of some examples. I have already dealt with simple sentences like 'Tom loves Mary' on page 77, so here I will focus on complex sentences.

The following sentence is an example of a universally quantified sentence, that is, a sentence making a claim about all objects of a certain sort:

All frogs are amphibians.

First, I will determine its logical form. It is clearly a universal claim that is to be parsed as outlined on page 81:

For all x (if x is a frog, then x is an amphibian)

The expression in brackets contains the standard connective 'if ..., then ...', so it can be further parsed as follows:

For all x (if (x is a frog), then (x is an amphibian))

Both 'x is a frog' and 'x is an amphibian' are enclosed in brackets; they contain no connectives and are not quantified. 'Is a frog' and 'is an amphibian' are then formalized by two distinct predicate letters P^1 and Q^1, respectively. So '(x is a frog)' becomes Px (omitting the arity-index); and 'x is an amphibian' becomes Qx. The expression 'for all' becomes the universal quantifier $\forall$, and 'if ..., then ...', the arrow $\rightarrow$. So, the formalization is

$$\forall x\, (Px \rightarrow Qx),$$

with the following dictionary:

P: ... is a frog

Q: ... is an amphibian

All universal claims can be formalized this way. Completely un-restricted universal claims are rare, but philosophers occasionally do make claims like the following, that are meant to be completely general:

Everything is material.

This sentence can be formalized as $\forall x\, Rx$, where R stands for 'is material'.

Existential claims are usually formalized by the existential quantifier; restrictions to a certain kind of objects is expressed by conjunction. Therefore, 'There are poisonous frogs' has the following logical form:

(R) There is at least one x ((x is a frog) and (x is poisonous))

The formalization is

$$\exists x (Px \wedge Q_1 x)$$

with the following dictionary:

P: ... is a frog

Q_1:   ... is poisonous

The English phrase 'No ... is ....' can be taken to be a negated existential quantification. The sentence

No frog is poisonous

can be rephrased as

It is not the case that there are poisonous frogs.

'It is not the case that' is a standard connective and it is formalized as $\neg$. I have already shown how to go about formalizing 'There are poisonous frogs'. So the sentence 'No frog is poisonous' is formalized as the following sentence, with the same dictionary as above:

$$\neg \exists x (Px \wedge Q_1 x) \tag{4.2}$$

Alternatively, one could have rephrased the original sentence 'No frog is poisonous' as the following sentence:

All frogs are non-poisonous.

This formalizes into $\forall x\,(Px \rightarrow \neg Q_1 x)$. This sentence and the alternative formalization (4.2) are logically equivalent under the semantics I will expound in Chapter 5. Both formalizations are equally sound.

The formalization of the following sentence requires two quantifiers:

Every student has a computer.

This is clearly a universal claim; so in the first step one obtains:

For all x (if x is a student, then x has a computer)

This is not yet the full logical form of the sentence: 'x has a computer' contains an existential claim and can be further analysed as

there is at least one y (x has y and y is a computer)

Now 'x has y' and 'y is a computer' cannot be further analysed and so they are put in brackets:

there is at least one y ((x has y) and (y is a computer))

Thus the full logical form of 'Every student has a computer' is

For all x (if (x is a student), then there is at least one y
((x has y) and (y is a computer)))

The formalization is now straightforward:

$$\forall x\,(Px \rightarrow \exists y\,(Rxy \wedge Qy))$$

The dictionary is specified in the following way:

P: ... is a student
Q: ... is a computer
R: ... has ...

The dictionary must always provide translations of all sentence letters, predicate letters, and constants occurring in the formalization. However, the dictionary must not contain translations for the variables. Variables in sentences never refer to particular objects; they are only used for making universal or existence claims.

Here is a somewhat more complicated example:

> If it's raining, then Bill reads a book or a newspaper

> (If (it's raining), then there is at least one x ((Bill reads x) and ((x is a book) or (x is a newspaper)))

The proper name 'Bill' is translated as a constant; the sentence 'It's raining' is translated as a sentence letter:

$$P \rightarrow \exists x \, (P^2 ax \wedge (Qx \vee Rx))$$

I have dropped the outer brackets according to Bracketing Convention 1. In the dictionary I have restored all arity-indices. In particular, one must avoid any confusions between the sentence letter (0-place predicate letter) P and the 2-place predicate letter P^2.

P: it's raining
Q^1:   ... is a book
R^1:   ... is a newpaper
P^2:   ... reads ...

Ternary predicate letters are needed for formalizing sentences such as the following:

> There is a country between Spain and France.

The logical form of this sentence is

> There is at least one x ((x is a country) and (x is between Spain and France))

By formalizing this, one obtains the following sentence of predicate logic:

$$\exists x \, (Px \wedge Qxbc)$$

The dictionary is as follows:

> P: ... is a country
> Q: ... is between ... and ...
> b: Spain
> c: France

Using the techniques outlined so far, one can formalize fairly complicated sentences. There are, however, some problem cases. Before discussing more intricate problems of formalization in Chapter 7, I shall introduce the semantics of predicate logic. Without having discussed the semantics of $\mathcal{L}_2$ first, it would be difficult to judge the soundness of translations between English and the language $\mathcal{L}_2$.

5 The Semantics of Predicate Logic

Discussions in metaphysics and in other areas in philosophy have been spurred by investigations into semantics. Whereas the semantics of the language $\mathcal{L}_1$ of propositional logic is somewhat crude and philosophically not very exciting, the semantics of the language $\mathcal{L}_2$ of predicate logic touches upon questions that are at the core of old debates in metaphysics.

In this chapter I shall confine myself to the technical core of the semantics of $\mathcal{L}_2$. The philosophical issues will resurface in later discussions about translating English sentences into sentences of $\mathcal{L}_2$. The technical account that I am going to present can be traced back to Tarski (1936) and subsequent work by Tarski, although I will deviate from Tarski's original approach in many details and in my notation. Tarski's definition of truth had a profound influence on many areas not only in philosophy, but also in mathematical logic, linguistics, and computer science.

In English, phrases such as 'Paris' or 'Julius Caesar', which are usually formalized as constants, and predicate expressions such as 'is tired' or 'loves', have fixed meanings. In the language $\mathcal{L}_2$ of predicate logic, the constants and predicate letters will not be assigned fixed meanings. This is not because it is not possible to assign fixed meanings to them, but rather because the validity of arguments or the property of being logically true do not depend on the particular meanings of constants and predicate letters. A sentence of the language $\mathcal{L}_2$ will be defined to be logically true, for instance, if and only if it is true under any interpretation of the constants and predicate letters. Thus any particular interpretations of constants and predicate letters do not matter for logical truth. A similar remark applies to validity: an argument in $\mathcal{L}_2$ will be

94

defined to be valid if and only if there is no interpretation under which the premises are all true and the conclusion is false. Thus, again, the validity of an argument does not depend on any specific interpretation we could assign to the constants and predicate letters.

As in the case of propositional logic, the notion of an interpretation from Characterization 1.9 will be made precise by the notion of a structure: structures provide interpretations for the non-logical, subject-specific vocabulary, that is, for predicate letters and constants. The interpretation that is assigned to a symbol by a structure is called the 'semantic value' or the 'extension' of the symbol in the structure.

5.1 STRUCTURES

The semantics of the language $\mathcal{L}_2$ will be given in the few definitions in italics in this chapter. The bulk of the chapter is only an attempt to motivate and elucidate these definitions.

I start by looking back at the semantics of the language $\mathcal{L}_1$ of propositional logic: whether a sentence of the language $\mathcal{L}_1$ is true depends on the truth or falsity of the sentence letters in that sentence. The truth-values of all the sentence letters are given by an $\mathcal{L}_1$-structure. Then the truth tables of the connectives allow one to calculate the truth-values of sentences formed with connectives.

Structures for predicate logic are more complicated: $\mathcal{L}_2$-structures need to determine more than merely the truth-values of sentence letters because the language $\mathcal{L}_2$ contains also other symbols, namely predicate letters and constants. $\mathcal{L}_2$-structures assign semantic values to these symbols as well. Sentence letters will receive truth-values as their semantic values in the same way as in propositional logic, but predicate letters will be assigned semantic values of a different kind.

Whether a sentence of $\mathcal{L}_2$ is true or false does not only depend on the semantic values of the constants and the sentence and predicate letters, but also on which objects the quantifiers are taken to range over. This situation is similar to English: the truth-value of the English sentence 'All glasses are empty' depends in part on whether the expression 'all glasses' is taken to range only over the glasses on a particular table or in a particular room or over all glasses in the world. The sentence is usually uttered when one is talking about particular glasses.

Thus, one of the things that an $\mathcal{L}_2$-structure does is specify a domain of discourse, which is just some non-empty set of objects. There are no restrictions on the domain of discourse except that it must not be empty.[1] If $\mathcal{A}$ is an $\mathcal{L}_2$-structure, I will write $D_\mathcal{A}$ for the structure's domain of discourse.

In the language $\mathcal{L}_2$, the constants play a role comparable to proper names in English, and in English proper names refer to objects: the English proper name 'Rome' refers to (or 'denotes') the capital of Italy, 'Volker Halbach' refers to Volker Halbach, and so on. Thus, an $\mathcal{L}_2$-structure assigns elements of the domain of discourse to the constants as their semantic values.

Sentence letters are treated as in propositional logic: they receive truth-values, that is, either T or F, as semantic values in an $\mathcal{L}_2$-structure. Hence, an $\mathcal{L}_2$-structure contains also an $\mathcal{L}_1$-structure.

Unary (1-place) predicate letters correspond to English expressions such as 'is green', 'walks', or 'is a philosopher'. Unary predicate letters have sets as their semantic values. The predicate letter P^1, for instance, can have as its semantic value the set of all green objects (or the set of all walking objects, or the set of all philosophers, or the empty set). On page 16, sets were conceived of as unary relations; so predicate letters have unary relations as semantic values, and an $\mathcal{L}_2$-structure must assign unary relations to unary predicate letters.

Binary predicate letters correspond to expressions such as 'loves' or 'is bigger than'. Binary predicate letters are interpreted by binary

---

1 Empty domains are not allowed in the traditional accounts of semantics for predicate logic. Admitting the empty domain would make the semantics for $\mathcal{L}_2$ more clumsy, but it is perfectly possible to admit them. From a philosophical point of view it would probably be more satisfying to admit the empty domain, but I want to avoid the additional technical complications, and I shall therefore follow the traditional account. The effects of the exclusion of the empty domain will be explained below by means of examples.

relations, that is, by sets of ordered pairs. The predicate letter P^2, for instance, can have the relation of loving, that is, the set of all ordered pairs $\langle d, e \rangle$ such that d loves e, as its semantic value. Thus, an $\mathcal{L}_2$-structure must assign binary relations to binary predicate letters as their semantic values.

Analogously, 3-place predicate letters are interpreted by 3-place relations, that is, sets of triples, and generally predicate letters with arity n are assigned n-ary relations (see Section 1.4).

In the following list I summarize which objects are assigned to expressions of $\mathcal{L}_2$ by an $\mathcal{L}_2$-structure as their semantic values or 'extensions'.

$\mathcal{L}_2$-expression	semantic value
constant	object
sentence letter	truth-value
unary predicate letter	set, unary relation
binary predicate letter	binary relation (= set of ordered pairs)
predicate letter of arity 3	3-place relation (= set of triples)
$\vdots$	$\vdots$

In sum, an $\mathcal{L}_2$-structure specifies a non-empty set as domain of discourse, it assigns elements of the domain to constants, it assigns a truth-value to every sentence letter, and it assigns an n-ary relation to every n-ary predicate letter.

The definition of an $\mathcal{L}_2$-structure can be spelled out more precisely in technical terms. I mention this definition only for the sake of those readers who want the full story. I shall not make use of this definition in what follows.

DEFINITION 5.1 ($\mathcal{L}_2$-STRUCTURE). *An $\mathcal{L}_2$-structure is an ordered pair $\langle D, I \rangle$ where D is some non-empty set and I is a function from the set of all constants, sentence letters, and predicate letters such that the value* *of every constant is an element of D, the value of every sentence letter is a truth-value* T *or* F, *and the value of every n-ary predicate letter is an n-ary relation.*

One might wonder why variables are not mentioned in the definition of an $\mathcal{L}_2$-structure. But just as 'he' does not stand for a particular object in the general claim 'If a reader is perplexed, he stops reading', a bound variable does not stand for a particular object in a sentence of $\mathcal{L}_2$. For this reason, $\mathcal{L}_2$-structures do not assign semantic values to variables.

For technical reasons, however, it is convenient to have semantic values not only for sentences but also for formulae with occurrences of free variables. Formulae with occurrences of free variables will also be assigned truth-values as semantic values. Whether a formula like P^1x with an occurrence of a free variable will receive the truth-value T or F depends on what the variables stand for in the same way 'He stops reading' is true or false for some persons but not for others. More than one variable may occur freely in a formula of $\mathcal{L}_2$: whether the formula $R^2xy \wedge R^1z$ receives the truth-value T or F depends on what the variables x, y, and z stand for. In addition to $\mathcal{L}_2$-structures, I therefore introduce a list that assigns an object to every variable of $\mathcal{L}_2$. This list affects only the truth or falsity of formulae with occurrences of free variables, but it does not affect the truth or falsity of sentences (that is, formulae with no free variables).

A variable assignment over an $\mathcal{L}_2$-structure $\mathcal{A}$ assigns an element of the domain D_A of $\mathcal{A}$ to each variable.[2] Occasionally I will drop the specification 'over the $\mathcal{L}_2$-structure $\mathcal{A}$', when it is clear from the context which $\mathcal{L}_2$-structure is meant.

Informally, one can picture a variable assignment as an infinite table with two lines that has all variables as entries in the first line, and elements of the domain of discourse as entries in the other line (as long

---

2 More formally, one can take a variable assignment over D to be a function from the set of all variables into D.

as one has names for all of them). For instance, there is a variable assignment α over an $\mathcal{L}_2$-structure with the set of all European cities as
domain, that assigns Paris to x and y, Rome to y_1 and z_1, Berlin to z,
London to x_1, Oslo to x_2. The assignment α assigns elements to all further variables, but of course I cannot specify an infinite list here. The
beginning of the variable assignment α may be visualized as follows:

x	y	z	x_1	y_1	z_1	x_2	
Paris	Paris	Berlin	London	Rome	Rome	Oslo	...

An $\mathcal{L}_2$-structure $\mathcal{A}$ and a variable assignment over $\mathcal{A}$ together assign semantic values to every variable, constant, sentence letter, and
predicate letter. *I will write* $|e|_{\mathcal{A}}^{\alpha}$ *for the semantic value of the expression e
in the $\mathcal{L}_2$-structure $\mathcal{A}$ under the variable assignment α over $\mathcal{A}$.* Thus, for
any $\mathcal{L}_2$-structure $\mathcal{A}$ and any variable assignment α over $\mathcal{A}$ the semantic
values of the respective $\mathcal{L}_2$-expressions are as follows:

(i) For any constant t, $|t|_{\mathcal{A}}^{\alpha}$ is the object in the domain $D_{\mathcal{A}}$ of $\mathcal{A}$ as-
signed to t by $\mathcal{A}$.

(ii) For any variable v, $|v|_{\mathcal{A}}^{\alpha}$ is the object in $D_{\mathcal{A}}$ assigned to the vari-
able v by the variable assignment α.

(iii) For any sentence letter Φ, $|\Phi|_{\mathcal{A}}^{\alpha}$ is the truth-value (either T or F)
assigned to Φ by $\mathcal{A}$.

(iv) For any unary predicate letter Φ, $|\Phi|_{\mathcal{A}}^{\alpha}$ is the unary relation, that
is, the set, assigned to Φ by $\mathcal{A}$.

(v) For any binary predicate letter Φ, $|\Phi|_{\mathcal{A}}^{\alpha}$ is the binary relation, that
is, the set of ordered pairs, assigned to Φ by $\mathcal{A}$.

(vi) For any 3-ary predicate letter Φ, $|\Phi|_{\mathcal{A}}^{\alpha}$ is the 3-ary relation, that
is, the set of ordered triples, assigned to Φ by $\mathcal{A}$.

And so on for predicate letters of higher arity.[3]

---

3 Therefore, if $\mathcal{A}$ is the ordered pair $\langle D, I \rangle$, then for all constants, and sentence and pred-
icate letters Φ, $|\Phi|_{\mathcal{A}}^{\alpha} = I(\Phi)$. This is what is expressed by (i) and (iii)–(vi).

5.2 TRUTH

The function $|\ldots|^\alpha_\mathcal{A}$ gives semantic values for all variables, constants, sentence letters, and predicate letters. In this section, $|\ldots|^\alpha_\mathcal{A}$ will be extended to cover complex formulae as well, that is, formulae that are not mere sentence letters.

The definition in which truth-values are assigned to formulae with connectives and quantifiers will be inductive. That is, first I shall define $|\ldots|^\alpha_\mathcal{A}$ for atomic formulae (Definition 4.5), and then I shall define the semantic values of formulae containing connectives and quantifiers. Any formula of $\mathcal{L}_2$ is either true or false in an $\mathcal{L}_2$-structure $\mathcal{A}$ under a variable assignment α over the $\mathcal{L}_2$-structure $\mathcal{A}$. Thus, for any formula ϕ either $|\phi|^\alpha_\mathcal{A} = $ T or $|\phi|^\alpha_\mathcal{A} = $ F obtains (but not both). $|\phi|^\alpha_\mathcal{A} = $ T is often read as 'α satisfies ϕ in $\mathcal{A}$'.[4] This use of the term 'satisfies' is motivated by its use in figures of speech like 'the property *of being red* is satisfied by the apple' or 'the equation $x^2 = y$ is satisfied by 3 and 9'; the only difference is that α is not a single object but rather an entire sequence of objects providing semantic values for all variables.

The truth-value of atomic formulae, that is, of formulae such as P^1b or R^2xc, is defined in the following way: P^1b, for instance, is true if and only if the object assigned to b is in the extension (semantic value) of P^1, that is, if $|b|^\alpha_\mathcal{A}$ is an element of the set $|P^1|^\alpha_\mathcal{A}$. Similarly, R^2xc is true if and only if the ordered pair $\langle |x|^\alpha_\mathcal{A}, |c|^\alpha_\mathcal{A} \rangle$, that is, the ordered pair with the value of x as its first component and the extension of c as its second component, is in the extension of R^2, that is, in the relation $|R^2|^\alpha_\mathcal{A}$. Therefore, the variable assignment α impinges on the truth-values of formulae with free occurrences of variables, such as R^2xc, because $|x|^\alpha_\mathcal{A}$ is given by the variable assignment α.

In the sentence P^1a the unary predicate letter P^1 receives a unary relation, that is, some set, as its extension (semantic value). I shall assume that $|P^1|^\alpha_\mathcal{A}$ is the set {Rome, London, Paris} and $|a|^\alpha_\mathcal{A}$ is Rome. On

---

4 Many authors prefer to write $\mathcal{A} \vDash \phi[\alpha]$ or something similar to express that α satisfies the formula ϕ in $\mathcal{A}$.

that assumption, P^1a is true because Rome is in the set {Rome, London, Paris}, that is, $|a|^\alpha_\mathcal{A} \in |P^1|^\alpha_\mathcal{A}$. The case of unary predicate letters is covered by the following clause because $|a|^\alpha_\mathcal{A}$ is the same as $\langle|a|^\alpha_\mathcal{A}\rangle$ according to the assumption on page 16 where it has been stipulated that d and $\langle d\rangle$ are the same for any object d.

   (i) $|\Phi t_1 \ldots t_n|^\alpha_\mathcal{A} = T$ if and only if $\langle|t_1|^\alpha_\mathcal{A}, \ldots, |t_n|^\alpha_\mathcal{A}\rangle \in |\Phi|^\alpha_\mathcal{A}$, where Φ is an n-ary predicate letter (n must be 1 or higher), and each of $t_1, \ldots, t_n$ is either a variable or a constant.

Thus, this clause determines whether a variable assignment satisfies a formula like P^1a, P^1x, R^2xy, R^3_2xxa, or Q^3xcy in a structure.

   If a formula is built up by means of connectives from other sentences, then truth-values can be assigned to this formula in the style of the Definition 2.6 of truth in an $\mathcal{L}_1$-structure: for instance, if the $\mathcal{L}_2$-formulae ϕ and ψ both have semantic value T, then the formula $\phi \wedge \psi$ should also have truth-value T; otherwise it should have F as its extension (semantic value). Thus, a variable assignment α satisfies the formula $\phi \wedge \psi$ in an $\mathcal{L}_2$-structure, if and only if α satisfies ϕ and ψ in that structure. Similarly a variable assignment α satisfies a formula $\neg\phi$ in an $\mathcal{L}_2$-structure, if and only if α does not satisfy ϕ itself in the structure. This can be expressed more formally by the following two definitional clauses:

   (ii) $|\neg\phi|^\alpha_\mathcal{A} = T$ if and only if $|\phi|^\alpha_\mathcal{A} = F$.
   (iii) $|\phi \wedge \psi|^\alpha_\mathcal{A} = T$ if and only if $|\phi|^\alpha_\mathcal{A} = T$ and $|\psi|^\alpha_\mathcal{A} = T$.

The clauses (iv)–(vi) for the remaining three connectives $\vee$, $\rightarrow$, and $\leftrightarrow$ are similar and will be listed below.

   It remains to define the semantic value, that is, the truth-value, of quantified formulae from the semantic values of shorter formulae. That is, I want to find clauses analogous to (ii) and (iii) for quantifiers. As an example I consider the following $\mathcal{L}_2$-formula:

$$\exists x\, Rxy$$

When should a variable assignment α satisfy this formula in a structure $\mathcal{A}$?

Assume, for instance, that the variable assignment α looks like this:

x	y	z	x_1	y_1	z_1	x_2	
Paris	Paris	Berlin	London	Rome	Rome	Oslo	...

In this case $|y|^\alpha_{\mathcal{A}}$ is Paris.

Assuming that R is translated as '... is smaller than ...', the formula $\exists x\, Rxy$ corresponds to the English phrase 'There is something smaller than it'. The pronoun 'it' plays the role of the variable y that occurs freely in $\exists x\, Rxy$. Now 'There is something smaller than it' is satisfied by Paris (which is assigned to y by α) if there is something smaller than Paris, that is, if there is something (for 'it$_1$') satisfying 'it$_1$ is smaller than it$_2$' when 'it$_2$' is taken to stand for Paris.

One can express this more precisely and perspicuously in terms of variable assignments for the formal language $\mathcal{L}_2$: the variable assignment α satisfies $\exists x\, Rxy$ if and only if there is a variable assignment β satisfying Rxy that differs from α at most in what is assigned to x. There is such a variable assignment β, assuming that $|R|^\alpha_{\mathcal{A}}$ is a relation containing, for instance, the pair $\langle$Oslo, Paris$\rangle$:

x	y	z	x_1	y_1	z_1	x_2	
Oslo	Paris	Berlin	London	Rome	Rome	Oslo	...

This variable assignment differs from α only in the entry for x. Since there is such a variable assignment, α satisfies the formulae $\exists x Rxy$ (in a structure $\mathcal{A}$ where $\langle$Oslo, Paris$\rangle$ is an element of the extension $|R|^\alpha_{\mathcal{A}}$ of R).

Of course the variable assignment β must not differ in the entry for y, as the question is whether the variable assignment α satisfies $\exists x Rxy$, that is, whether $\exists x Rxy$ is true when y is taken to stand for Paris.

In the general case, a variable assignment α satisfies a formula $\exists x\phi$ if and only if there is a variable assignment β satisfying ϕ that differs from α at most in the entry for x. ϕ may have free occurrences of other variables than y; for this reason β must agree with α on all variables with the possible exception of x.

So I define for all variables v and formulae ϕ:

(viii) $|\exists v \, \phi|^{\alpha}_{\mathcal{A}} = \mathrm{T}$ if and only if $|\phi|^{\beta}_{\mathcal{A}} = \mathrm{T}$ for at least one variable assignment β over $\mathcal{A}$ differing from α in v at most.

By saying that α differs from β in v at most, I mean that $|u|^{\alpha}_{\mathcal{A}} = |u|^{\beta}_{\mathcal{A}}$ for all variables u with the possible exception of v. Hence, in terms of tables, a variable assignment α and a variable assignment β differ in a given variable v at most, if they agree in all columns with the possible exception of the column for the variable v. The two tables above are an example of two variable assignments differing in x.

Universal quantifiers can be treated in a similar way. When should one say, for instance, that a variable assignment α satisfies the formula $\forall y \, (Rxy \wedge Ryz)$ in a structure $\mathcal{A}$? That is, when should the following obtain?

$$|\forall y \, (Rxy \wedge Ryz)|^{\alpha}_{\mathcal{A}} = \mathrm{T}$$

$\forall y$ expresses generality. α will satisfy $\forall y \, (Rxy \wedge Ryz)$ in $\mathcal{A}$ if and only if everything in the domain of $\mathcal{A}$ will make $Rxy \wedge Ryz$ true if it is taken to stand for y (with the values of x and z unchanged from α). Thus, α satisfies $\forall y \, (Rxy \wedge Ryz)$ in $\mathcal{A}$ if and only if every β that differs from α only in y satisfies $Rxy \wedge Ryz$ in $\mathcal{A}$.

This can be generalized to all variables v and $\mathcal{L}_2$-formulae ϕ: a variable assignment α satisfies a formula $\forall v \phi$ in a structure $\mathcal{A}$ if and only if every variable assignment β that differs from α at most in v satisfies ϕ. Of course, only variable assignments over $\mathcal{A}$ are considered: the variable assignments can only assign objects from the domain of $\mathcal{A}$ to the variables.

The general clause can now be stated as follows:

(vii) $|\forall v \, \phi|^{\alpha}_{\mathcal{A}} = \mathrm{T}$ if and only if $|\phi|^{\beta}_{\mathcal{A}} = \mathrm{T}$ for all variable assignments β over $\mathcal{A}$ differing from α in v at most.

I will now collect the different clauses into a definition of satisfaction. Given an $\mathcal{L}_2$-structure, this definition determines for any variable assignment α and any $\mathcal{L}_2$-formula whether α satisfies ϕ in $\mathcal{A}$, that is, whether $|\phi|^{\alpha}_{\mathcal{A}} = \mathrm{T}$ or $|\phi|^{\alpha}_{\mathcal{A}} = \mathrm{F}$.

DEFINITION 5.2 (SATISFACTION). *Assume $\mathcal{A}$ is an $\mathcal{L}_2$-structure, α is a variable assignment over $\mathcal{A}$, ϕ and ψ are formulae of $\mathcal{L}_2$, and v is a variable. For a formula ϕ either $|\phi|_{\mathcal{A}}^{\alpha} = $ T or $|\phi|_{\mathcal{A}}^{\alpha} = $ F obtains. Formulae other than sentence letters then receive the following semantic values:*

   (i) *$|\Phi t_1 \ldots t_n|_{\mathcal{A}}^{\alpha} = $ T if and only if $\langle |t_1|_{\mathcal{A}}^{\alpha}, \ldots, |t_n|_{\mathcal{A}}^{\alpha} \rangle \in |\Phi|_{\mathcal{A}}^{\alpha}$, where Φ is a n-ary predicate letter (n must be 1 or higher), and each of $t_1, \ldots, t_n$ is either a variable or a constant.*

  (ii) *$|\neg\phi|_{\mathcal{A}}^{\alpha} = $ T if and only if $|\phi|_{\mathcal{A}}^{\alpha} = $ F.*

 (iii) *$|\phi \wedge \psi|_{\mathcal{A}}^{\alpha} = $ T if and only if $|\phi|_{\mathcal{A}}^{\alpha} = $ T and $|\psi|_{\mathcal{A}}^{\alpha} = $ T.*

 (iv) *$|\phi \vee \psi|_{\mathcal{A}}^{\alpha} = $ T if and only if $|\phi|_{\mathcal{A}}^{\alpha} = $ T or $|\psi|_{\mathcal{A}}^{\alpha} = $ T.*

  (v) *$|\phi \rightarrow \psi|_{\mathcal{A}}^{\alpha} = $ T if and only if $|\phi|_{\mathcal{A}}^{\alpha} = $ F or $|\psi|_{\mathcal{A}}^{\alpha} = $ T.*

 (vi) *$|\phi \leftrightarrow \psi|_{\mathcal{A}}^{\alpha} = $ T if and only if $|\phi|_{\mathcal{A}}^{\alpha} = |\psi|_{\mathcal{A}}^{\alpha}$.*

(vii) *$|\forall v\, \phi|_{\mathcal{A}}^{\alpha} = $ T if and only if $|\phi|_{\mathcal{A}}^{\beta} = $ T for all variable assignments β over $\mathcal{A}$ differing from α in v at most.*

(viii) *$|\exists v\, \phi|_{\mathcal{A}}^{\alpha} = $ T if and only if $|\phi|_{\mathcal{A}}^{\beta} = $ T for at least one variable assignment β over $\mathcal{A}$ differing from α in v at most.*

In general, what α assigns to variables not occurring freely in a formula ϕ does not impinge on whether α satisfies ϕ in $\mathcal{A}$. So, if $|\phi|_{\mathcal{A}}^{\alpha} = $ T, and if β is a variable assignment differing from α only in variables that do not occur freely in ϕ, then also $|\phi|_{\mathcal{A}}^{\beta} = $ T. In particular, the variable v does not occur freely in a formula of the form $\exists v\, \psi$. Thus, α satisfies $\exists v\, \psi$ in $\mathcal{A}$ independently of what α assigns to the variable v. A similar remark applies to formulae with a universal quantifier.

If ϕ is a sentence, that is, if no variable occurs freely in ϕ then $|\phi|_{\mathcal{A}}^{\alpha}$ does not depend on the variable assignment α in any way at all. Hence, if ϕ is a sentence, then $|\phi|_{\mathcal{A}}^{\alpha}$ is the same truth-value as $|\phi|_{\mathcal{A}}^{\beta}$ for all variable assignments β over $\mathcal{A}$.

In order to simplify the notation one may drop the index for the variable assignment and write $|\phi|_{\mathcal{A}}$ if ϕ is a sentence. In general, one can drop the variable assignment when the semantic value is the same for all variable assignments. This is the case for constants, sentence letters, predicate letters, and sentences.

Truth in an $\mathcal{L}_2$-structure is now defined in terms of satisfaction:

DEFINITION 5.3 (TRUTH). *A sentence ϕ is true in an $\mathcal{L}_2$-structure $\mathcal{A}$ if and only if $|\phi|_{\mathcal{A}}^{\alpha} = T$ for all variable assignments α over $\mathcal{A}$.*

As pointed out above, the truth-value of a sentence in a structure is the same for all variable assignments. Therefore, if a sentence is satisfied (in a structure) by some variable assignment, it will be satisfied by all variable assignments. Consequently, a sentence ϕ is true in an $\mathcal{L}_2$-structure $\mathcal{A}$ if and only if $|\phi|_{\mathcal{A}}^{\alpha} = T$ for at least one variable assignment α over $\mathcal{A}$.

The Definition 5.3 of truth has generated and continues to generate extensive discussion. The views on its philosophical value differ wildly. At any rate, Definition 5.3 has been a big success as a tool in philosophy, mathematics, computer science, and linguistics. The extent to which this definition can also be adapted to natural languages such as English is also a matter of some controversy.

As an example I will consider a specific $\mathcal{L}_2$-structure, which I call $\mathcal{E}$. Its domain of discourse is the set of all European cities. It assigns the set {Florence, Stockholm, Barcelona} to Q^1, the relation of *being smaller than* to R^2, Florence to a, and London to b. This information can be displayed in the following way:

$$|Q^1|_{\mathcal{E}} = \{\text{Florence, Stockholm, Barcelona}\}$$
$$|R^2|_{\mathcal{E}} = \{\, \langle d, e \rangle \colon d \text{ is smaller than } e \,\}$$
$$|a|_{\mathcal{E}} = \text{Florence}$$
$$|b|_{\mathcal{E}} = \text{London}$$

Thus, $|R^2|_{\mathcal{E}}$ is the set {⟨Florence, London⟩, ⟨Berlin, London⟩, ⟨Warsaw, London⟩, ⟨Florence, Birmingham⟩, ... }.

I have dropped the index for the variable assignment and written $|Q^1|_{\mathcal{E}}$ rather than $|Q^1|_{\mathcal{E}}^{\alpha}$ since variable assignments do not affect the semantic values of predicate letters and constants.[5]

---

5 What is assigned to other constants, sentence, and predicate letters is irrelevant for the

EXAMPLE 5.4. The sentence R^2ab is true in $\mathcal{E}$.

Proof. Since Florence is smaller than London, the pair ⟨Florence, London⟩ is an element of the relation of *being smaller than*, and I can reason as follows (the comments to the right explain what justifies the proof step on the left):

⟨Florence, London⟩ $\in \{ \langle d, e \rangle: d$ is smaller than $e \}$

$\langle |a|_\mathcal{E}, |b|_\mathcal{E} \rangle \in |R^2|_\mathcal{E}$ definition of $\mathcal{E}$

$|R^2ab|_\mathcal{E} = T$ Definition 5.2(i)

This shows that R^2ab is true in $\mathcal{E}$.   □

EXAMPLE 5.5. The sentence $\forall x\,(Q^1x \to R^2xb)$ is true in $\mathcal{E}$.

Proof. Let α be an arbitrary variable assignment. There are two cases:
     First case: $|x|^\alpha_\mathcal{E}$ is in $|Q^1|_\mathcal{E}$, that is, $|x|^\alpha_\mathcal{E}$ is either Florence, Stockholm, or Barcelona. As all three cities are smaller than London, and $|b|_\mathcal{E}$ is London, one has the following:

$\langle |x|^\alpha_\mathcal{E}, |b|_\mathcal{E} \rangle \in |R^2|_\mathcal{E}$

$|R^2xb|^\alpha_\mathcal{E} = T$ Definition 5.2(i)

$|Q^1x \to R^2xb|^\alpha_\mathcal{E} = T$ Definition 5.2(v)

     Second case: $|x|^\alpha_\mathcal{E}$ is not in $|Q^1|_\mathcal{E}$. In this case one can proceed as follows:

$|x|^\alpha_\mathcal{E}$ is not in $|Q^1|_\mathcal{E}$

$|Q^1x|^\alpha_\mathcal{E} = F$ Definition 5.2(i)

$|Q^1x \to R^2xb|^\alpha_\mathcal{E} = T$ Definition 5.2(v)

following. For the sake of definiteness, I could stipulate that $\mathcal{E}$ assigns the empty set as extension to all predicate letters other than Q^1 and R^2, T to all sentence letters, and Rome to all constants other than a and b.

Therefore, in both cases, that is, for every variable assignment α over $\mathcal{E}$, the following obtains:

$$|Q^1 x \rightarrow R^2 xb|_{\mathcal{E}}^{\alpha} = \text{T}.$$

Consequently, according to Definition 5.2(vii), $|\forall x\, (Q^1 x \rightarrow R^2 xb)|_{\mathcal{E}}^{\beta} = \text{T}$ for every variable assignment β. Hence, by Definition 5.3, the sentence $\forall x\, (Q^1 x \rightarrow R^2 xb)$ is true in $\mathcal{E}$. $\qquad\square$

The final example sentence contains two quantifiers.

EXAMPLE 5.6. The sentence $\forall x\, \exists y\, (R^2 xy \vee R^2 yx)$ is true in $\mathcal{E}$.

Proof. Let α be an arbitrary variable assignment over $\mathcal{E}$.

First case: $|x|_{\mathcal{E}}^{\alpha}$ is not London (the largest city in Europe). Then change the entry for y into London (if it is not already London) and call the resulting variable assignment β. By definition, β differs from α in y at most. Since every European city except London itself is smaller than London, one has the following:

$$\langle |x|_{\mathcal{E}}^{\beta}, |y|_{\mathcal{E}}^{\beta} \rangle \in |R^2|_{\mathcal{E}}$$

$|R^2 xy|_{\mathcal{E}}^{\beta} = \text{T}$	Definition 5.2(i)
$|R^2 xy \vee R^2 yx|_{\mathcal{E}}^{\beta} = \text{T}$	Definition 5.2(iv)
$|\exists y\, (R^2 xy \vee R^2 yx)|_{\mathcal{E}}^{\alpha} = \text{T}$	Definition 5.2(viii)

The last line holds because β differs from α at most in y.

Second case: $|x|_{\mathcal{E}}^{\alpha}$ is London. Change the entry for y in α into Florence (or any other European city smaller than London), and call this variable assignment β; it differs from α only in y. The first of the following lines holds because $|y|_{\mathcal{E}}^{\beta}$ is Florence, which is smaller than $|x|_{\mathcal{E}}^{\alpha}$, that is, London:

$$\langle |y|_{\mathcal{E}}^{\beta}, |x|_{\mathcal{E}}^{\beta} \rangle \in |R^2|_{\mathcal{E}}$$

$|R^2 yx|_{\mathcal{E}}^{\beta} = \text{T}$	Definition 5.2(i)

$$|R^2xy \vee R^2yx|_{\mathcal{E}}^{\beta} = T \qquad \text{Definition 5.2(iv)}$$

$$|\exists y\,(R^2xy \vee R^2yx)|_{\mathcal{E}}^{\alpha} = T \qquad \text{Definition 5.2(viii)}$$

The last line holds, because α differs from β in y at most.

Therefore, I have proved that $|\exists y(R^2xy \vee R^2yx)|_{\mathcal{E}}^{\alpha} = T$ for any variable assignment α over $\mathcal{E}$. According to Definition 5.2(vii) this implies

$$|\forall x \exists y\,(R^2xy \vee R^2yx)|_{\mathcal{E}} = T,$$

which shows that the sentence is true in $\mathcal{E}$. ☐

In practice hardly anyone will go through all these steps explicitly. The foregoing examples should have illustrated how the semantics for the language of predicate logic works and how the truth or falsity of all sentences is determined by an $\mathcal{L}_2$-structure.

5.3 VALIDITY, LOGICAL TRUTHS, AND CONTRADICTIONS

With the definition of truth in hand one can now define such notions as logical truth, contradiction, the validity of an argument, and so on. The following definition is analogous to Definition 2.7 for propositional logic.

DEFINITION 5.7.

(i) *A sentence ϕ of $\mathcal{L}_2$ is logically true if and only if ϕ is true in all $\mathcal{L}_2$-structures.*

(ii) *A sentence ϕ of $\mathcal{L}_2$ is a contradiction if and only if ϕ is not true in any $\mathcal{L}_2$-structure.*

(iii) *A sentence ϕ and a sentence ψ are logically equivalent if both are true in exactly the same $\mathcal{L}_2$-structures.*

(iv) *A set Γ of $\mathcal{L}_2$-sentences is semantically consistent if and only if there is an $\mathcal{L}_2$-structure $\mathcal{A}$ in which all sentences in Γ are true. As in propositional logic, a set of $\mathcal{L}_2$-sentences is semantically inconsistent if and only if it is not semantically consistent.*

Also, the definition of validity of an argument in $\mathcal{L}_2$ follows the pattern set out in the definition of validity of an argument in propositional logic, that is, in Definition 2.9.

DEFINITION 5.8. *Let Γ be a set of sentences of $\mathcal{L}_2$ and ϕ a sentence of $\mathcal{L}_2$. The argument with all sentences in Γ as premisses and ϕ as conclusion is valid if and only if there is no $\mathcal{L}_2$-structure in which all sentences in Γ are true and ϕ is false.*

This just captures the intuitive idea that an argument is valid if and only if any $\mathcal{L}_2$-structure that makes the premisses true also makes the conclusion true.

That the argument with all sentences in Γ as premisses and ϕ as conclusion is valid, is abbreviated as $\Gamma \vDash \phi$. This is also expressed by saying that the sentences in Γ (logically) imply ϕ or by saying that ϕ follows (logically) from the sentences in Γ. The symbol $\nvDash$ is the negation of $\vDash$; so, it is defined as follows: $\Gamma \nvDash \phi$ if and only if not $\Gamma \vDash \phi$.

I have not excluded the possibility that there is no premiss at all in an argument. So, Γ may be the empty set. If Γ is the empty set and $\Gamma \vDash \phi$, one may also simply write $\vDash \phi$. As I have said above, $\Gamma \vDash \phi$ means that ϕ is true in all $\mathcal{L}_2$-structures in which all sentences in Γ are true. Now if there are no sentences in Γ, one has $\Gamma \vDash \phi$ if and only if ϕ is true in all structures. Consequently, $\vDash \phi$ means that ϕ is true in all $\mathcal{L}_2$-structures tout court; that is, it means that ϕ is logically true.

I introduce a further notational convention, already adopted for propositional logic: When the sentences in Γ are written out explicitly, the set brackets around the sentences may be dropped: For instance, one may write

$$\forall x\, Qx, \ \forall x\, (Qx \rightarrow Rx) \ \vDash \ \exists x\, Rx$$

rather than the following:

$$\big\{\forall x\, Qx, \ \forall x\, (Qx \rightarrow Rx)\big\} \vDash \exists x\, Rx$$

5.4 COUNTEREXAMPLES

How can one show that an argument is valid? And how can one show that it is not valid?

For the language $\mathcal{L}_1$ of propositional logic, these question are usually easily answered (if there are not too many or too long sentences involved): One can check out whether an argument in $\mathcal{L}_1$ is valid by means of a truth table.

In the language $\mathcal{L}_2$, it is much harder to show that an argument is valid or not. There is not a finite set of possibilities one can check out in order to find out whether an argument is valid or not. There are infinitely many domains of discourse, and even a single binary predicate letter can be interpreted by infinitely many binary relations. Showing that an $\mathcal{L}_2$-argument is valid by proving that the conclusion is true in all $\mathcal{L}_2$-structures in which all the premises are true is, therefore, usually a difficult task. A more efficient and elegant way of establishing that an argument in $\mathcal{L}_2$ is valid will be introduced in the next chapter.

In order to show that an argument is not valid, however, one does not have to prove something about all $\mathcal{L}_2$-structures; one has only to find an $\mathcal{L}_2$-structure in which all premises of the argument are true and its conclusion is false. Such $\mathcal{L}_2$-structures are called counterexamples. In this section I will explain how to use counterexamples to disprove the validity of arguments.

An $\mathcal{L}_2$-structure $\mathcal{A}$ is a counterexample to an argument if and only if all premises of the argument are true in $\mathcal{A}$ and the conclusion is false in $\mathcal{A}$.

As explained above, a sentence is logically valid if and only if the argument with no premises and the sentence as its conclusion is valid. Thus, one can use counterexamples to show that a sentence is not logically true:

An $\mathcal{L}_2$-structure is a counterexample to an $\mathcal{L}_2$-sentence if the sentence is not true in it. An $\mathcal{L}_2$-sentence is logically true if and only if there are no counterexamples to it.

I will prove the following claim by means of a counterexample.

EXAMPLE 5.9. The sentence $Qb \rightarrow \forall x\, Qx$ is not logically true.

In order to find a counterexample to this sentence, one could reason informally as follows: b could satisfy Q, but other objects might not satisfy Q and thus $\forall x\, Qx$ would be false. One can turn this into a proof. First, an $\mathcal{L}_2$-structure with a domain of discourse containing at least two objects is required. And then, the object that is the semantic value of b needs to be in the set that is the semantic value of Q, while one of the other objects is not in this set. Now this can be turned into a proper proof of the claim that $Qb \rightarrow \forall x\, Qx$ is not logically true:

Proof. Let $\mathcal{B}$ be an $\mathcal{L}_2$-structure with the set $\{1,2\}$ as its domain of discourse and the following semantic values for Q and b:[6]

$$|Q|_{\mathcal{B}} = \{1\},$$
$$|b|_{\mathcal{B}} = 1.$$

I will now show that $Qb \rightarrow \forall x\, Qx$ receives the semantic value F in this $\mathcal{L}_2$-structure. Let α be the variable assignment that assigns 2 to every variable, so $|x|^{\alpha}_{\mathcal{B}} = 2$. Now one can reason as follows, using $\notin$ as an abbreviation for 'is not an element of':

$2 \notin \{1\}$	
$|x|^{\alpha}_{\mathcal{B}} \notin |Q|_{\mathcal{B}}$	definition of α and $\mathcal{B}$
$|Qx|^{\alpha}_{\mathcal{B}} = F$	Definition 5.2(i)
$|\forall x\, Qx|^{\alpha}_{\mathcal{B}} = F$	Definition 5.2(vii)
$1 \in \{1\}$	
$|b|_{\mathcal{B}} \in |Q|_{\mathcal{B}}$	definition of $\mathcal{B}$
$|Qb|^{\alpha}_{\mathcal{B}} = T$	Definition 5.2(i)
$|Qb \rightarrow \forall x\, Qx|^{\alpha}_{\mathcal{B}} = F$	Definition 5.2(v)

---

6 For the sake of definiteness I should specify also the value of other constants, sentence, and predicate letters. But as they do not make a difference to the truth-values of sentences, I will not specify them in this and the following examples.

By the Definition 5.3 of truth, $Qb \to \forall x\, Qx$ is not true in $\mathcal{B}$ and thus, according to Definition 5.7(i), $Qb \to \forall x\, Qx$ is not logically true. □

In order to show that $Qb \to \forall x\, Qx$ is not logically true, I could have employed objects other than the numbers 1 and 2. The two numbers are convenient because of their short names. There is no need to use more fancy objects. Generally, it is sensible to keep things simple by choosing small domains of discourse. In some cases, however, it may be necessary to use large domains; there are even cases where the domain has to be infinite.

Next I will turn to an argument and show that $\forall x\, \exists y\, Rxy$ does not logically imply $\exists y\, \forall x\, Rxy$.

EXAMPLE 5.10. $\forall x\, \exists y\, Rxy \nvDash \exists y\, \forall x\, Rxy$.

The premiss could be the translation of a sentence such as 'For everything there is something with the same mass'; the conclusion would then be the translation of 'There is something that has the same mass as any object'. If there are exactly two things differing in mass, then 'For everything there is something with the same mass' is true, because every object agrees with itself in its mass, and the conclusion is false, because the mass of neither of the two objects matches the mass of the other object. Hence, one can use an $\mathcal{L}_2$-structure with a domain containing exactly two objects. R needs to have a relation as extension that relates every object to itself but not to the other object in the domain.

Proof. The $\mathcal{L}_2$-structure $\mathcal{C}$ is defined as follows:

$$D_\mathcal{C} = \{\text{the sun, the moon}\}$$
$$|R|_\mathcal{C} = \{\langle\text{the sun, the sun}\rangle, \langle\text{the moon, the moon}\rangle\}$$

First I will show that the premiss is true in the $\mathcal{L}_2$-structure $\mathcal{C}$. Let α be an arbitrary variable assignment over $\mathcal{C}$. Then change the value of x so that the values of x and y are the same, that is, change the entry for x into the sun if $|y|_\mathcal{C}^\alpha$ is the sun and into the moon if $|y|_\mathcal{C}^\alpha$ is the moon; call the resulting variable assignment β. The first line in the following proof, then, holds in virtue of the definition of $|R|_C$, and because $|x|_C^\beta = |y|_C^\beta$.

$$\langle |x|_C^\beta, |y|_C^\beta \rangle \in |R|_C$$
$$|Rxy|_C^\beta = \text{T} \qquad\qquad \text{Definition 5.2(i)}$$
$$|\exists y\, Rxy|_C^\beta = \text{T} \qquad\qquad \text{Definition 5.2(viii)}$$
$$|\forall x\, \exists y\, Rxy|_C^\alpha = \text{T} \qquad\qquad \text{Definition 5.2(vii)}$$

The last line holds because the foregoing reasoning applies to all variable assignments α. Hence, the premiss is true in C.

It remains to show that the conclusion is false in C. Assume to the contrary that $\exists y\, \forall x\, Rxy$ is true in C. Then, by Definition 5.2(viii), there is a variable assignment α such that the following holds:

$$|\forall x\, Rxy|_C^\alpha = \text{T}.$$

Thus, by Definition 5.2(vii),

$$|Rxy|_C^\beta = \text{T}$$

for every variable assignment β that differs from α at most in x. But this is not the case since one can choose a variable assignment β such that $|x|_C^\beta$ is different from $|y|_C^\beta$ and so $\langle |x|_C^\beta, |y|_C^\beta \rangle$ is not in $|R|_C$.

Since the premiss is true in C and the conclusion is false in C, the argument is not valid. $\qquad\qquad\square$

EXAMPLE 5.11. $\forall x\, (Px \to Qx \vee Rx),\ Pa \nvDash Ra.$

To motivate the counterexample below one can reason as follows: If there is a counterexample – call it D – the premiss Pa must be true in D, and so $|a|_D$ must be in $|P|_D$. The premiss $\forall x(Px \to Qx \vee Rx)$ therefore implies that $|a|_D$ is either in $|Q|_D$ or in $|R|_D$. So if the premiss is to be true at least one of the latter must be the case. As the conclusion Ra must be false, $|a|_D$ must not be in $|R|_D$, and, therefore, $|a|_D$ must be an element of $|Q|_D$. So, one can employ a counterexample with a single object in its domain, where that object is in the extensions of P and Q while the extension of R is the empty set:

Proof. The following $\mathcal{L}_2$-structure is a counterexample:

$$D_\mathcal{D} = \{1\},$$
$$|a|_\mathcal{D} = 1,$$
$$|P|_\mathcal{D} = \{1\},$$
$$|Q|_\mathcal{D} = \{1\},$$
$$|R|_\mathcal{D} = \emptyset.$$

There is only one variable assignment over $\mathcal{D}$ because its domain $D_\mathcal{D}$ contains only one object and every variable is assigned the number 1. Therefore, $|x|_\mathcal{D}^\alpha = 1$ for all variable assignments α. To show that the first premiss is true, one can reason as follows:

$1 \in \{1\}$
$|x|_\mathcal{D}^\alpha \in |Q|_\mathcal{D}$ definitions of α and $\mathcal{D}$
$|Qx|_\mathcal{D}^\alpha = \text{T}$ Definition 5.2(i)
$|Qx \vee Rx|_\mathcal{D}^\alpha = \text{T}$ Definition 5.2(iv)
$|Px \rightarrow Qx \vee Rx|_\mathcal{D}^\alpha = \text{T}$ Definition 5.2(v)

Since this holds for all variable assignments over $\mathcal{D}$, as α is the only such variable assignment, $\forall x\, (Px \rightarrow Qx \vee Rx)$ is true in $\mathcal{D}$.

The second premiss is also true in $\mathcal{D}$:

$1 \in \{1\}$
$|a|_\mathcal{D} \in |P|_\mathcal{D}$ definitions of $\mathcal{D}$
$|Pa|_\mathcal{D} = \text{T}$ Definition 5.2(i)

The conclusion, however, is false in $\mathcal{D}$:

$1 \notin \emptyset$
$|a|_\mathcal{D} \notin |R|_\mathcal{D}$ definitions of $\mathcal{D}$
$|Ra|_\mathcal{D} = \text{F}$ Definition 5.2(i)

This shows that both premisses are true and that the conclusion is false in $\mathcal{D}$. Therefore, the argument is not valid. □

6 Natural Deduction

A valid argument need not be obviously valid. One can establish the validity of such an argument by breaking it into smaller arguments and by showing that one can pass from the premisses to the conclusion through a sequence of small and obvious steps. That is, one proves the conclusion from the premisses via intermediate conclusions: the original premisses are used to derive obvious conclusions, which in turn are employed in the next step as premisses to derive further conclusions, and so on, until the original conclusion is obtained. Such a sequence of obvious arguments is called a 'proof'.

Whether a step is obvious depends on the perspective. However, one might try to show that there is a fixed list of simple proof rules that are sufficient for establishing the validity of any valid argument. The rules should be formulated in a way that makes it easy to check whether any given step in a proof conforms to one of these rules. If a set of rules that can be used in proofs is fixed, then there cannot be a serious disagreement about the admissibility of any given step in a proof, and there is an objective notion of proof.

For the languages of propositional and of predicate logic one can provide such a list of admissible rules that legitimate steps in a proof.

It is obvious for which arguments there should be proofs: first, there should be proofs for valid arguments only. Formally speaking, it must not be possible to pass from the premisses in a set Γ to a sentence ϕ, if it is not the case that $\Gamma \vDash \phi$. The rules must be sound in this sense. Second, the proof rules should be complete in the sense that there should be proofs for all valid arguments: if $\Gamma \vDash \phi$, then it should be possible to reach ϕ from the premisses in Γ by going through proof steps that conform to the rules for proofs.

In order to show that $\Gamma \vDash \phi$, one can then simply give a proof rather than argue using $\mathcal{L}_2$-structures as in the previous chapter. This will greatly facilitate establishing the validity of arguments in predicate logic.

Logicians have devised different proof systems for different purposes: Some systems are easy to implement on computers, others are very easy to state (but hard to work in), still others facilitate general investigations into the notion of provability. I will employ a system that enables one to use proof steps that are not dissimilar to the steps people take in everyday reasoning. The rules I will specify should be intuitively plausible, but not every intuitively sound step is a permissible rule in the system: the system has not been designed to be as efficient as possible. It is devised to show that any proof can be broken down into simple and elementary steps of very few types. If the objective were a very efficient proof system, more rules would have to be added.

Because the proof rules are fairly close to proof steps used in informal proofs, systems of the kind described in this chapter are called Natural Deduction systems. They were introduced independently by Jaśkowski (1934) and Gentzen (1935). The system I am going to present is a variation of Gentzen's version.

Proofs in Natural Deduction start with an assumption. Any sentence can be assumed:

> assumption rule   *The occurrence of a sentence ϕ with no sentence above it is an assumption. An assumption of ϕ is a proof of ϕ.*

It may seem somewhat odd that the solitary occurrence of a sentence is already a proof, but it is convenient to consider a line with a single sentence ϕ as a proof of ϕ from the assumption ϕ, because this makes the following definitions more straightforward.

Every proof begins with assumptions. The further rules for proofs show how to extend a proof, that is, how to form longer and longer proofs by adding further sentences. When stating the rules I will talk about 'appending' sentences to already existing proofs. By this I mean the following: one appends a sentence ϕ to a proof by drawing a horizontal line under the proof and then writing ϕ under this line. One appends a sentence ϕ to two (or three) proofs by writing the proofs side by side, then drawing a single line under all of these proofs, and then writing ϕ under that single line.

All the rules enable one to append only a single sentence in a given step. Thus, in every proof there is always a single sentence ϕ at the bottom (or the 'root') of the proof. The proof is a proof of this sentence ϕ. Proofs have therefore the shape of (upward-branching) trees.

For each connective and quantifier there is an introduction rule and an elimination rule. I shall use abbreviations: for instance, '∧Intro' is short for '∧-introduction rule'.

6.1 PROPOSITIONAL LOGIC

For the sake of those who are concentrating just on propositional logic, I shall only use examples in $\mathcal{L}_1$ in this section. Nonetheless, the rules apply equally to predicate logic.

I will start with the rules for conjunction:

∧Intro   *The result of appending $\phi \wedge \psi$ to a proof of ϕ and a proof of ψ is a proof of $\phi \wedge \psi$.*

Graphically, this rule allows one to write a proof ending with ϕ and a proof ending with ψ side by side, to draw a horizontal line below both, and to write $\phi \wedge \psi$ under this line. Thus an application of the rule will have the following shape:

$$\frac{\phi \qquad \psi}{\phi \wedge \psi} \text{ ∧Intro}$$

The assumptions in the proof of $\phi \wedge \psi$ are all the assumptions in the proofs of ϕ and ψ, respectively, because any assumption in the proof of ϕ or ψ, that is, any sentence with no other formula above it in the proofs of ϕ or ψ, will also be an assumption in the proof of $\phi \wedge \psi$, that is, it will not have a sentence above it in the proof of $\phi \wedge \psi$.

The order of the proofs of ϕ and ψ does not matter. The rule does not require that the proof of ϕ is written to the left. So an application of $\wedge$Intro can also look like this:

$$\frac{\begin{matrix} \vdots & \vdots \\ \psi & \phi \end{matrix}}{\phi \wedge \psi} \ \wedge\text{Intro}$$

The same applies to other rules: in rules where a sentence is appended to two (or in one case three) proofs, the rules allow one to write down the proofs in any order.

For $\wedge$ there are two elimination rules:

$\wedge$Elim1   *The result of appending ϕ to a proof of $\phi \wedge \psi$ is a proof of ϕ.*

The other rule allows one to keep ψ:

$\wedge$Elim2   *The result of appending ψ to a proof of $\phi \wedge \psi$ is a proof of ψ.*

The two rules can be depicted as follows:

$$\frac{\begin{matrix} \vdots \\ \phi \wedge \psi \end{matrix}}{\phi} \ \wedge\text{Elim1} \qquad\qquad \frac{\begin{matrix} \vdots \\ \phi \wedge \psi \end{matrix}}{\psi} \ \wedge\text{Elim2}$$

The first rule allows one to drop the second part of the conjunction, the second rule allows one to drop the first part.

With these rules in hand I can already construct a proof. First, I will assume $(P \wedge Q) \wedge R$. The rule $\wedge$Elim1 allows me to append $P \wedge Q$ to the proof, and $\wedge$Elim2 allows me to append Q to the resulting proof. So I can obtain a proof of Q under the assumption $(P \wedge Q) \wedge R$:

$$\frac{\dfrac{(P \wedge Q) \wedge R}{P \wedge Q} \ \wedge\text{Elim1}}{Q} \ \wedge\text{Elim2}$$

The labels '∧Elim1' and '∧Elim2' do not belong to the proof; they are mere comments that are intended to help the reader to grasp the proof. Occasionally, when I think that the labels will facilitate understanding, I will add them.

Next I shall specify rules for the arrow →. In order to motivate the introduction rule for the arrow, I will look at how one might establish a claim of the form 'if ..., then ...' like the following:

(A) If CO_2-emissions are not being cut, temperatures will rise globally.

To derive the conclusion, one will use additional assumptions about climate change, the greenhouse effect, and so on, which I will not specify here. Using these additional assumptions, one could argue as follows for (A):

> Assume that CO_2-emissions are not being cut. Then the CO_2-level in the atmosphere ... [now one uses the additional assumption, probably talking about the greenhouse effect, and concludes:] so temperatures will rise globally. Therefore, if CO_2-emissions are not being cut, temperatures will rise globally.

One makes the assumption that CO_2-emissions are not being cut only in order to show that in that case temperatures will rise globally. This assumption is made only for the sake of the argument and once (A) has been concluded, one is no longer assuming that CO_2-emissions are not being cut. The proof of (A) is based only on the additional assumptions about climate change etc., but not on the assumption that CO_2-emissions are not being cut. Thus, when one concludes (A), one does not make the assumption anymore that CO_2-emissions are not being cut; one claims only that temperatures will rise if CO_2-emissions are not being cut without assuming anything about whether the emissions are cut or not. Logicians describe this by saying that, when one concludes (A), one has 'discharged' the assumption that CO_2-emissions are not being cut.

In any case one can argue for a claim of the form 'If *A*, then *B*' by proving *B* from the assumption *A* in the following way: one proves *B* by assuming *A*; then one concludes 'If *A*, then *B*' without assuming *A* anymore.

In Natural Deduction the rule for introducing the arrow works in the same way: one assumes a sentence ϕ, derives a sentence ψ from it, and then the rule allows one to conclude $\phi \to \psi$ and to get rid of or 'discharge' the assumption of ϕ.

Square brackets are used to indicate that an assumption has been discharged:

> *In formal proofs, assumptions are discharged by surround-*
> *ing them with square brackets.*

Of course one must only discharge assumptions in accordance with the rules.

The proof technique used in the above informal proofs is captured by the introduction rule for $\to$:

$\to$Intro   *The result of appending $\phi \to \psi$ to a proof of ψ*
and discharging all assumptions of ϕ in the proof of ψ is a
proof of $\phi \to \psi$.

So one may add $\phi \to \psi$ to a proof with ψ at the root and then enclose all assumptions of ϕ (that is, all occurrences of ϕ with no line above them) in the proof of ψ in square brackets.

The graphical representation looks like this:

$$\begin{array}{c} [\phi] \\ \vdots \\ \psi \\ \hline \phi \to \psi \end{array} \to\text{Intro}$$

This rule does not require that the proof of ψ actually contains an assumption of ϕ. Only if there are any assumptions of ϕ in the proof of ψ, they must be discharged.

The rule for eliminating $\to$ is straightforward:

→Elim   *The result of appending* ψ *to a proof of* ϕ *and a proof of* $\phi \to \psi$ *is a proof of* ψ.

This rule is graphically represented as follows:

$$\frac{\phi \quad\quad \phi \to \psi}{\psi} \;\to\text{Elim}$$

This rule is also called 'modus ponens'.

Before giving some examples, I will introduce a new piece of notation:

DEFINITION 6.1. *The sentence* ϕ *is provable from* Γ *(where* Γ *is a set of* $\mathcal{L}_2$-*sentences) if and only if there is a proof of* ϕ *with only sentences in* Γ *as non-discharged assumptions. The phrase '*ϕ *is provable from* Γ*' is abbreviated as* $\Gamma \vdash \phi$. *If* Γ *is empty,* $\Gamma \vdash \phi$ *is abbreviated as* $\vdash \phi$. *If* Γ *contains exactly the sentences* $\psi_1, \ldots, \psi_n$, *one may write* $\psi_1, \ldots, \psi_n \vdash \phi$ *instead of* $\{\psi_1, \ldots, \psi_n\} \vdash \phi$.

EXAMPLE 6.2. $\vdash P \land Q \to P$.

Proof. I show step by step how to establish this claim. First, $P \land Q$ is assumed:

$$P \land Q$$

Applying $\land$Elim1 yields the following:

$$\frac{P \land Q}{P} \;\land\text{Elim1}$$

The rule →Intro allows one to add $P \land Q \to P$ and to discharge $P \land Q$:

$$\frac{\dfrac{[P \land Q]}{P}\;\land\text{Elim1}}{P \land Q \to P}\;\to\text{Intro}$$

All assumptions in this proof have been discharged. Thus, $P \land Q \to P$ is provable from the empty set of premises, that is, $\vdash P \land Q \to P$.   □

This is a typical proof of a sentence of the form $\phi \to \psi$: usually one assumes ϕ, arrives through some steps at ψ, and then uses →Intro to derive $\phi \to \psi$ and to discharge any assumptions of ϕ.

The introduction rules for disjunction are as follows:

∨Intro1   *The result of appending a sentence $\phi \lor \psi$ to a proof of ϕ is a proof of $\phi \lor \psi$.*

As in the case for the elimination rules for ∧, there is also another introduction rule for ∨:

∨Intro2   *The result of appending a sentence $\phi \lor \psi$ to a proof of ψ is a proof of $\phi \lor \psi$.*

The graphical representations are as follows:

$$
\begin{array}{c} \vdots \\ \phi \\ \hline \phi \lor \psi \end{array} \text{∨Intro1} \qquad\qquad \begin{array}{c} \vdots \\ \psi \\ \hline \phi \lor \psi \end{array} \text{∨Intro2}
$$

The elimination rule for ∨ is somewhat tricky. It corresponds to the following informal proof strategy:

Assume 'A or B' is given. Then one can try to prove C by making a case distinction: First, one tries to derive C assuming A; then one tries to derive C assuming B. If C can be derived in both cases, then (given 'A or B') one may conclude C.

This type of reasoning – reasoning by drawing the same conclusion from both parts of a disjunction – is captured in the following rule:

∨Elim   *The result of appending χ to a proof of $\phi \lor \psi$, a proof of χ, and another proof of χ, and of discharging all assumptions of ϕ in the first proof of χ and of discharging all assumptions of ψ in the second proof of χ, is a proof of χ.*

An application of ∨Elim looks like this:

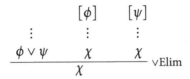

$$\frac{\phi \vee \psi \qquad \chi \qquad \chi}{\chi} \text{ vElim}$$

In the first proof of χ only assumptions of ϕ are discharged; one must not discharge assumptions of ψ in this proof when applying the rule. Of course, this remark applies analogously to the second proof of χ. The rule may look somewhat awkward because from two proofs of χ one only obtains another, longer proof of χ. The point of the rule is that the assumptions of ϕ and ψ can be discharged, so that χ now follows from $\phi \vee \psi$ without assuming ϕ or ψ.

   In an actual proof one would proceed as follows: assume one has a proof of $\phi \vee \psi$. Then, one will start a new branch by assuming ϕ and another new branch by assuming ψ. After obtaining χ on both branches, one can discharge all assumptions of ϕ in the first proof of χ, and all assumptions of ψ in the second proof of χ, and append χ to the three proofs.

   I will illustrate the use of vElim with the following example.

EXAMPLE 6.3. $P \vee Q, P \rightarrow R \vdash R \vee Q.$

Proof.

In the last step – an application of vElim – the assumptions P and Q are discharged.   □

   The introduction rule for negation is another rule that allows one to discharge assumptions. The underlying strategy is as follows: If one can derive a contradiction from an assumption of A, then one may conclude: 'It is not the case that A.' This rule is called 'reductio ad absurdum' (reduction to an absurdity).

¬Intro   *The result of appending a sentence ¬φ to a proof
of ψ and a proof of ¬ψ and of discharging all assumptions
of φ in both proofs is a proof of ¬φ.*

Schematically, the rule for ¬-introduction has the following shape:

$$\frac{\begin{array}{cc} [\phi] & [\phi] \\ \vdots & \vdots \\ \psi & \neg\psi \end{array}}{\neg\phi} \text{ ¬Intro}$$

I will demonstrate the use of the rule with an example:

EXAMPLE 6.4. $\neg(P \rightarrow Q) \vdash \neg Q$.

Proof. In order to arrive at a conclusion of the form ¬φ, it is often useful to assume φ and to try to derive a contradiction. In this case I will assume Q and try to obtain a contradiction with the only premiss, viz, $\neg(P \rightarrow Q)$.

$$\frac{\dfrac{[Q]}{P \rightarrow Q} \text{ →Intro} \qquad \neg(P \rightarrow Q)}{\neg Q} \text{ ¬Intro}$$

In the left branch of the proof I have applied →Intro even though there is no assumption of P. This is in accordance with the formulation of →Intro: nothing in →Intro actually requires that there is actually an assumption of P; only if there are any, they must be discharged.   □

The rule of negation elimination allows one to discharge assumptions of negated sentences:[1]

---

1 This rule allows for non-constructive indirect proofs. For instance, the formula φ could be an existence claim. Negation elimination allows one to conclude the existence of an object with a certain property from the inconsistency of the assumption that there isn't any object with that property. Thus one will be able to prove that an object satisfying a certain property exists, without being able to show directly, of any particular object, that it has this property. If one is interested in constructive proofs, that is, proofs that

¬Elim   *The result of appending a sentence ϕ to a proof of ψ and a proof of $\neg\psi$ and of discharging all assumptions of $\neg\phi$ in both proofs is a proof of ϕ.*

Graphically an application of the rule looks like this:

$$
\begin{array}{cc}
[\neg\phi] & [\neg\phi] \\
\vdots & \vdots \\
\psi & \neg\psi \\
\end{array}
$$
$$
\underline{\qquad\qquad\qquad} \text{ ¬Elim}
$$
$$
\phi
$$

Here is an example showing how the negation elimination rule can be used:

EXAMPLE 6.5. $\neg P \to Q, \neg Q \vdash P$.

$$
\cfrac{\cfrac{[\neg P] \quad \neg P \to Q}{Q}{\scriptstyle\to\text{Elim}} \qquad \neg Q}{P}{\scriptstyle\neg\text{Elim}}
$$

Negation elimination can be used to prove the *law of excluded middle*:

EXAMPLE 6.6. $\vdash P \vee \neg P$.

The proof is surprisingly awkward. One cannot prove one of the sentences P or $\neg P$ (without assumptions) and then apply ∨Intro1 or ∨Intro2. Rather one proves $P \vee \neg P$ indirectly by assuming $\neg(P \vee \neg P)$,

require one to exhibit a particular example of an object that demonstrably has the property in question in order to prove the relevant existence claim, then the rule for negation elimination has to be dropped. The system that is obtained by replacing this rule with the weaker rule that allows one to go from ϕ and $\neg\phi$ to ψ is called 'intuitionistic logic'. It differs from classical Natural Deduction. The law of the excluded middle, $\phi \vee \neg\phi$ (Example 6.5), and the law of double negation elimination, $\neg\neg\phi \to \phi$, are some of the principles that are theorems of classical logic, which is the logic studied here, but not of intuitionistic logic. Tennant (1990) provides an introduction to intuitionistic logic with a proof system that is similar to the version of Natural Deduction used here.

which is then shown to lead to a contradiction. This makes it possible to apply the negation elimination rule.

Proof. First I assume P and apply $\vee$Intro1:

$$\frac{P}{P \vee \neg P} \; \vee\text{Intro1}$$

In the next step, I assume $\neg(P \vee \neg P)$, which is the negation of the sentence that is to be proved.

$$\frac{\dfrac{[P]}{P \vee \neg P} \; \vee\text{Intro1} \qquad \neg(P \vee \neg P)}{\neg P} \; \neg\text{Intro}$$

Now $\vee$Intro2 can be used:

$$\frac{\dfrac{\dfrac{[P]}{P \vee \neg P} \; \vee\text{Intro1} \qquad \neg(P \vee \neg P)}{\neg P} \; \neg\text{Intro}}{P \vee \neg P} \; \vee\text{Intro2}$$

Now $\neg(P \vee \neg P)$ is assumed again, so that $\neg$Intro can be applied once more. This time $\neg$Intro is used to discharge the assumption $\neg(P \vee \neg P)$, which occurs twice.

$$\frac{\dfrac{\dfrac{\dfrac{[P]}{P \vee \neg P} \; \vee\text{Intro1} \quad [\neg(P \vee \neg P)]}{\neg P} \; \neg\text{Intro}}{P \vee \neg P} \; \vee\text{Intro2} \qquad [\neg(P \vee \neg P)]}{P \vee \neg P} \; \neg\text{Elim}$$

□

The rules for the double arrow are modelled on the rules for the single arrow. Given a proof that would allow one to infer $\phi \rightarrow \psi$ by applying $\rightarrow$Intro and given a proof that would allow one to infer $\psi \rightarrow \phi$ by applying $\rightarrow$Intro, both proofs can be combined into a proof of $\phi \leftrightarrow \psi$ by applying the rule for introducing $\leftrightarrow$. At the same time those

assumptions that would have been discharged by the two applications
of →Intro are discharged. The rules for eliminating the double arrow
are very much like the rule for eliminating the single arrow with the
exception that one can also use the right-to-left direction of the double
arrow.

↔Intro   *The result of appending $\phi \leftrightarrow \psi$ to a proof of ψ*
and to a proof of ϕ and of discharging all assumptions of ϕ
in the proof ψ and all assumptions of ψ in the proof of ϕ is a
proof of $\phi \leftrightarrow \psi$.

↔Elim1   *The result of appending ψ to a proof of $\phi \leftrightarrow \psi$*
and a proof of ϕ is a proof of ψ.

↔Elim2   *The result of appending ϕ to a proof of $\phi \leftrightarrow \psi$*
and a proof of ψ is a proof of ϕ.

The graphical representations of the rules are as follows:

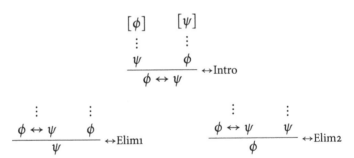

In the following proof I will illustrate the use of the introduction
rule for the double arrow.

EXAMPLE 6.7. $\vdash (P \rightarrow Q) \leftrightarrow (\neg Q \rightarrow \neg P)$.

Proof.

$$\frac{\dfrac{[P \to Q] \quad [P]}{Q} \; \text{¬Intro} \quad [\neg Q]}{\dfrac{\neg P}{\neg Q \to \neg P} \; \to\text{Intro}} \qquad \frac{\dfrac{[\neg Q \to \neg P] \quad [\neg Q]}{\neg P} \; \text{¬Elim} \quad [P]}{\dfrac{Q}{P \to Q} \; \to\text{Intro}}$$
$$(P \to Q) \leftrightarrow (\neg Q \to \neg P)$$

For the last line ↔Intro is used. ☐

In cases like the following it is often useful to start from the root and to consider how one might have obtained the sentence that is to be proved.

EXAMPLE 6.8. $\neg(Q \wedge \neg R) \vdash Q \to R$.

Proof.

$$\frac{\neg(Q \wedge \neg R) \qquad \dfrac{[Q] \quad [\neg R]}{Q \wedge \neg R}}{\dfrac{R}{Q \to R}}$$

The assumption $\neg(Q \wedge \neg R)$ is not bracketed; it remains as an undischarged assumption. Thus, $\neg(Q \wedge \neg R) \vdash Q \to R$ is established. ☐

Finally, I prove a variant of the 'ex falso quodlibet'-principle:

EXAMPLE 6.9. $P, \neg P \vdash Q$.

Proof. The following proof contains a surprising application of ¬Elim. The formula Q is introduced although $\neg Q$ has never been assumed. The rule ¬Elim allows one to introduce ϕ and to discharge all assumptions of $\neg\phi$ even if there are not any.

$$\frac{P \qquad \neg P}{Q} \; \text{¬Elim}$$

This application of ¬Elim complies with ¬Elim, as it is not a requirement that there actually be assumptions of $\neg\phi$. ☐

The following result says that the rules for Natural Deduction have been chosen in such a way that there are proofs for exactly those arguments in $\mathcal{L}_1$ that are valid.

THEOREM 6.10 (ADEQUACY FOR PROPOSITIONAL LOGIC). *Assume that ϕ and all elements of Γ are $\mathcal{L}_1$-sentences. Then $\Gamma \vdash \phi$ if and only if $\Gamma \vDash \phi$.*

I will not prove this theorem here.

In particular, if a sentence of $\mathcal{L}_1$ is a tautology (logically true), then there is a proof of that sentence without undischarged assumptions.

The adequacy result says that the rules given here are sufficient for proving a conclusion from premises if the argument is valid. Any rule that can be added is either not sound, that is, it allows one to prove sentences that are not logically true, or it is dispensable (but it may provide a short cut). I shall return to adequacy in more detail in Section 7.1; there adequacy will be discussed with respect to predicate logic.

6.2 PREDICATE LOGIC

The proof rules of propositional logic, which were expounded in the previous section, apply to all sentences including the sentences of $\mathcal{L}_2$. The following example contains sentences of the language $\mathcal{L}_2$ that are not in $\mathcal{L}_1$; but the proof requires only rules from propositional logic, that is, introduction and elimination rules for connectives.

EXAMPLE 6.11. $\vdash \neg(\forall x\, Px \lor \exists y\, Py) \to \neg\forall x\, Px$.

Proof. Since one wants to prove a sentence of the form $\phi \to \psi$, the ϕ, which corresponds to $\neg(\forall x\, Px \lor \exists y\, Py)$ in the present example, is assumed. From this assumption one tries to arrive at $\neg\forall x\, Px$. Since this is a negated sentence, one may hope to get it by using ¬Intro; so $\forall x\, Px$ is assumed. That is almost a contradiction: applying ∨Intro1 to $\forall x\, Px$ gives $\forall x\, Px \lor \exists y\, Py$, and the contradiction is obtained:

$$\neg(\forall x\, Px \lor \exists y\, Py) \qquad \frac{\forall x\, Px}{\forall x\, Px \lor \exists y\, Py}\ \text{∨Intro1}$$

Now ¬Intro is applied by appending ¬$\forall x\, Px$ to the two proofs and discharging the assumption $\forall x\, Px$:

$$\cfrac{\neg(\forall x\, Px \vee \exists y\, Py) \qquad \cfrac{\cfrac{[\forall x\, Px]}{\forall x\, Px \vee \exists y\, Py}\ \text{\scriptsize{}vIntro1}}{}}{\neg\forall x\, Px}\ \text{\scriptsize{}¬Intro}$$

One finishes the proof by applying →Intro:

$$\cfrac{\cfrac{[\neg(\forall x\, Px \vee \exists y\, Py)] \qquad \cfrac{\cfrac{[\forall x\, Px]}{\forall x\, Px \vee \exists y\, Py}\ \text{\scriptsize{}vIntro1}}{}}{\neg\forall x\, Px}\ \text{\scriptsize{}¬Intro}}{\neg(\forall x\, Px \vee \exists y\, Py) \rightarrow \neg\forall x\, Px}\ \text{\scriptsize{}→Intro}$$

All assumptions are discharged, so the claim is established. □

I will now turn to the rules for $\forall$ and $\exists$. First, I will explain the rule for eliminating $\forall$, which may be motivated by considering the following argument:

> If some person has made more than ten mistakes then that person won't pass. Therefore, if Ben has made more than ten mistakes he won't pass.

Here one is going from a universal claim to a claim about a specific instance. The rule for eliminating $\forall$, which is also known as 'universal instantiation'-rule, allows one to pass from a universally quantified sentence to a special instance. For instance, the rule licenses the step from the universally quantified sentence $\forall x\,(Px \rightarrow Qx)$ to the instance $Pa \rightarrow Qa$.

In order to give a general formulation of $\forall$Elim I employ the following definition:

DEFINITION 6.12. *Assume v is a variable, t a constant, and ϕ an $\mathcal{L}_2$-formula with at most v occurring freely. Then $\phi[t/v]$ is the sentence obtained by replacing all free occurrences of v in ϕ by t.*

For instance, $Px\,[b_2/x]$ is Pb_2; and $\forall y\,(Pxy \to \exists x\,Rxy)\,[b/x]$ is the sentence $\forall y\,(Pby \to \exists x\,Rxy)$. In the second case only the first occurrence of x has been replaced because the other two are bound occurrences.

The rule for eliminating the universal quantifier can now be stated as follows:

∀Elim   *The result of appending $\phi[t/v]$ to a proof of $\forall v\,\phi$*
is a proof of $\phi[t/v]$.

In this rule it is assumed that t is a constant, v a variable, and $\forall v\,\phi$ is a sentence (so that only v can occur freely in ϕ).

Thus an application of this rule has the following form:

$$\vdots$$
$$\frac{\forall v\,\phi}{\phi[t/v]}\ \ \forall\,\text{Elim}$$

Here, ϕ is an $\mathcal{L}_2$-formula in which only the variable v occurs freely; t is a constant.

Thus the rule allows one to drop the quantifier $\forall v$ at the beginning of a sentence and to replace all free occurrences of v in the resulting formula with the constant t.

The following example explains why only free occurrences of the variable are replaced:

$$\frac{\forall y\,(Py \wedge \exists y\,Qy)}{Pb_5 \wedge \exists y\,Qy}\ \ \forall\,\text{Elim}$$

If one were allowed to replace also the last occurrence of y, which is bound, one would to get to $Pb_5 \wedge \exists y Q b_5$, which is logically equivalent to $Pb_5 \wedge Qb_5$. This step is clearly not sound: from $\forall y(Py \wedge \exists y\,Qy)$ it does not follow that b_5 is Q. Intuitively speaking, only occurrences of y in $\forall y\,(Py \wedge \exists y\,Qy)$ that are 'caught' by the universal quantifier $\forall y$ can be replaced by the constant; the last occurrence of y belongs to the existential quantifier and must be left alone.

The introduction rule for the universal quantifier is more difficult to state. In order to argue for the general claim that every traveller's journey from London to Munich in 2007 took over two hours, one could reason as follows:

> Assume somebody travelled from London to Munich in 2007. Call him John Doe. If he took the train ... [now each means of transport is taken into account, and it is argued in every case that the journey must have taken more than two hours]. Therefore John Doe's journey took over two hours. Therefore, since John Doe is an arbitrary person, every traveller's journey from London to Munich in 2007 took over two hours.

The idea here is that one talks about a nondescript particular instance as an example using a name. In the story above, this nondescript instance is a person who is dubbed 'John Doe'. The name 'John Doe' is not used to name a specific real person. Then one carries out the argumentation for this instance, and concludes that this argument applies to every instance because the chosen instance was just used as an example. For the validity of the argument it is important that the chosen person is arbitrary and that one did not bring in any specific information about that person or object (if there is such a person or object at all).

The rule for introducing the universal quantifier in Natural Deduction works in a similar way: $\vdash \forall x(Px \rightarrow Px)$ will be established by taking an arbitrary constant, say, c (corresponding to the use of a name 'John Doe' above), and arguing as follows:

$$\frac{[Pc]}{Pc \rightarrow Pc} \rightarrow \text{Intro}$$

Since c was chosen to name a nondescript instance as an example, the claim also holds for every object. Now, one substitutes the variable x for the constant c in $Pc \rightarrow Pc$ and prefixes the universal quantifier $\forall x$ to the formula. Then one can add this sentence to the proof, in accordance with the rule for introducing $\forall$:

$$\frac{\dfrac{[Pc]}{Pc \rightarrow Pc} \text{→Intro}}{\forall x (Px \rightarrow Px)} \text{∀Intro}$$

In formulating the general rule ∀Intro, however, one must exercise caution. One might think that ∀Intro can be formulated in the following way: given a proof of a sentence ϕ, one replaces a constant in the sentence by a variable v, writes $\forall v$ in front of the sentence, and then appends the resulting sentence to the proof. However, such a rule would allow one to derive false conclusions from true premises for three reasons.

FIRST PROBLEM. I will illustrate the problem by considering the following attempted proof:

$$\text{(P)} \qquad \text{∀Elim} \frac{\dfrac{\forall y (Py \rightarrow \exists x\, Ryx)}{Pa \rightarrow \exists x\, Rax}}{\forall x (Px \rightarrow \exists x\, Rxx)} \text{ incorrect ∀-introduction}$$

If (P) were a correct proof one could derive $\forall x (Px \rightarrow \exists x Rxx)$ from $\forall y (Py \rightarrow \exists x\, Ryx)$. So (P) cannot be a correct proof: it would allow one to go from the formalization of 'Every student sees something' to the formalization of 'For every student there is something that sees itself'. The first sentence is true while the latter is false if there is at least one student and nothing can see itself.[2]

It should be obvious what went wrong. When the constant a was replaced by x in the sentence $Pa \rightarrow \exists x\, Rax$, the x replacing the last occurrence of a got 'caught' by the quantifier $\exists x$:

$$\forall x (Px \rightarrow \exists x\, Rx\underbrace{x})$$
$$\text{actual binding}$$

But of course the 'intention' was that the penultimate occurrence of x

---

2 The proof that there is a counterexample to the argument with $\forall y (Py \rightarrow \exists x\, Ryx)$ as premiss and $\forall x (Px \rightarrow \exists x Rxx)$ as conclusion is the content of Exercise 5.2(ii).

should refer back to the universal quantifier $\forall x$ and not to the existential quantifier:

$$\forall x \, (Px \rightarrow \exists x \, Rxx)$$

$$\underbrace{}$$

intended binding

The problem can be avoided in the following way: when one adds a sentence $\forall v \, \phi$ to a proof by applying the rule for introducing $\forall$ then the preceding sentence must be ϕ with all free occurrences of the variable v replaced by the constant t. In other words, the rule allows one to continue a proof ending with $\phi[t/v]$ by adding the sentence $\forall v \, \phi$. So the rule for introducing $\forall$ will take the following form (with some additional restrictions on occurrences of the constant t specified below):

$$\vdots$$
$$\frac{\phi[t/v]}{\forall v \, \phi}$$

In the above attempted proof (P), I passed from $Pa \rightarrow \exists x \, Rax$ to $\forall x \, (Px \rightarrow \exists x \, Rxx)$. But this step is not covered by the rule that licenses only the step from $\phi[t/v]$ to $\forall v \, \phi$: The result $(Px \rightarrow \exists x \, Rxx)[a/x]$ of replacing all free occurrences of x by a is the sentence $Pa \rightarrow \exists x \, Rxx$, not $Pa \rightarrow \exists x \, Rax$. Only going from $Pa \rightarrow \exists x \, Rxx$ to the sentence $\forall x \, (Px \rightarrow \exists x \, Rxx)$ would be covered by the rule.

SECOND PROBLEM. Assume one starts a proof by assuming Qb and then generalizes in the following way:

$$\frac{Qb}{\forall x \, Qx} \quad \text{incorrect } \forall\text{-introduction}$$

This is not correct. If it were correct, one could apply $\rightarrow$Intro in the next step:

$$\frac{\dfrac{[Qb]}{\forall x \, Qx} \quad \text{incorrect } \forall\text{-introduction}}{Qb \rightarrow \forall x \, Qx} \quad \rightarrow\text{Intro}$$

Thus, one would have proved that $\vdash Qb \rightarrow \forall x\, Qx$; but $Qb \rightarrow \forall x\, Qx$ is certainly not logically true, as has been shown in Example 5.9.

For this reason, one must make sure that one is not using any specific assumptions containing the constant that is used as an 'arbitrary example' over which one can generalize. So when $\forall$Intro is applied by going from $\phi[t/v]$ to $\forall v\, \phi$, the constant t must not occur in any undischarged assumption. In the discussion of the example of John Doe I said that it is important that the person chosen as an example (John Doe) is arbitrary. The restriction that the constant must not occur in any undischarged assumption is the formal counterpart of the requirement that John Doe is an 'arbitrary' person about whom one does not have any specific information.

In the earlier, correct proof of $\forall x\,(Px \rightarrow Px)$ the constant c occurred in the assumption Pc, but that assumption had been discharged by the time $\forall$Intro was applied. So this proof meets the restriction that c must not occur in any undischarged premiss when the universal quantifier is introduced.

THIRD PROBLEM. The following attempted proof meets all conditions that were imposed on applications of $\forall$Intro to avoid the first and second problem:

$$\frac{\dfrac{\forall y\, Ryy}{Raa}}{\forall x\, Rax}$$

However, the argument with $\forall y\, Ryy$ as premiss and $\forall x\, Rax$ as its conclusion is not valid: it would alow one to go from the formalization of 'Everything is self-identical' to the formalization of 'John is identical with everything'.[3] Thus, some condition must be imposed on the rule $\forall$Intro that blocks the step from Raa to $\forall x\, Rax$. This can be done by disallowing one to keep some occurrences of a in the sentence that is added in accordance with the rule. Only passing from Raa to $\forall x\, Rxx$ would be admissible. Thus, since an application of $\forall$Intro is a step from

---

3 The proof of $\forall y\, Ryy \nvDash \forall x\, Rax$ is Exercise 5.2(iii).

$\phi[t/v]$ to $\forall v\,\phi$, the rule $\forall$Intro can be applied only if ϕ (that is, the formula following the universal quantifier) does not contain the constant t, that is, if no occurrence of t is retained when $\forall$Intro is applied.

In the following formulation of the rule for introducing the universal quantifier all three problems are avoided:

> $\forall$Intro   *Assume that ϕ is a formula with at most v occurring freely and that ϕ does not contain the constant t. Assume further that there is a proof of $\phi[t/v]$ in which t does not occur in any undischarged assumption. Then the result of appending $\forall v\,\phi$ to that proof is a proof of $\forall v\,\phi$.*

The rule can be represented as follows:

$$\begin{array}{c} \vdots \\ \dfrac{\phi[t/v]}{\forall v\,\phi} \ \forall\text{Intro} \end{array}$$

provided the constant t does not occur in ϕ or in any undischarged assumption in the proof of $\phi[t/v]$.

In less formal terms, the restrictions on $\forall$Intro can be summed up in two points: First, one must make sure that one is not generalizing over a constant that occurs in an undischarged assumption or that is still in the sentence one tries to obtain. Second, in an application of the rule, one has to make sure that the variable of the newly introduced quantifier is not caught by a quantifier that is already in the formula.

In the case of the existential quantifier the introduction rule is the easy one:

> $\exists$Intro   *The result of appending $\exists v\,\phi$ to a proof of $\phi[t/v]$ is a proof of $\exists v\,\phi$.*

$$\dfrac{\phi[t/v]}{\exists v\,\phi} \ \exists\text{Intro}$$

Of course t is a constant, v a variable, and $\exists v\,\phi$ is an $\mathcal{L}_2$-sentence.

The rule for eliminating the existential quantifier is the most complicated rule. Consider the following argument:

There is at least one epistemologist. All epistemologists are
philosophers. Therefore, there is at least one philosopher.

The two premisses have $\exists x\, Px$ and $\forall x\,(Px \rightarrow Qx)$ as their respective
formalizations; the formalization of the conclusion is $\exists x\, Qx$. The dictionary has the following two entries:

> P: ... is an epistemologist
> Q: ... is a philosopher

The corresponding argument in $\mathcal{L}_2$ is valid. The question is how one
can *prove* the conclusion from the two premisses. If one could in some
way get Pc from the first premiss $\exists x\, Px$, the rest of the proof would be
obvious:

$$\frac{\quad Pc \quad \dfrac{\forall x\,(Px \rightarrow Qx)}{\dfrac{Pc \rightarrow Qc}{} \; \forall\text{Elim}}}{\dfrac{Qc}{\exists x\, Qx} \; \exists\text{Intro}} \; \rightarrow\text{Elim}$$

The problem is that Pc does not follow from $\exists x\, Px$. The premiss $\exists x\, Px$
just states that there is *some* epistemologist; it does not give one a specific epistemologist and, in particular, it does not give one a particular
name c for an epistemologist.

The conclusion $\exists x\, Qx$ does not say anything specific about c. In
the proof I could have used any other constant in place of c. So one
might apply the following proof strategy: one may *assume* Pc. This is
tantamount to picking an arbitrary name like 'John Doe' and assuming
that John Doe is an epistemologist. Once a sentence not containing c is
proved, one can discharge the assumption Pc using the premiss $\exists x\, Px$:
the conclusion does not depend any more on the assumption that c is
one of the P's.

$$\frac{\exists x\, Px \qquad \dfrac{[Pc] \qquad \dfrac{\dfrac{\forall x\,(Px \rightarrow Qx)}{Pc \rightarrow Qc}\;\forall\text{Elim}}{\dfrac{Qc}{\exists x\, Qx}\;\exists\text{Intro}}\;\rightarrow\text{Elim}}{}}{\exists x\, Qx}$$

The point in the last step of the proof is that the premiss Pc can be discharged, so one has now proved the conclusion from the existence claim $\exists x\, Px$ rather than from the specific instance Pc. Less formally speaking, the conclusion that there is a philosopher does not depend on the assumption that there is an epistemologist called 'John Doe'.

When making an assumption such as Pc one must not choose a constant about which one already has specific information: the constant acts as an 'arbitrary example' in the same way as in ∀Intro. The precise statement of the elimination rule for ∃ is so convoluted because the restrictions on the constant must ensure that the constant can play its role as an arbitrary label.

> ∃Elim   Assume that ϕ is a formula with at most v occur-
> ring freely and that the constant t does not occur in ϕ. As-
> sume further that there is a proof of the sentence ψ in which t
> does not occur in ψ or in any undischarged assumption other
> than $\phi[t/v]$. Then the result of appending ψ to a proof of $\exists v\, \phi$
> and the proof of ψ and of discharging all assumptions of $\phi[t/v]$
> in the proof of ψ is a proof of ψ.

As before, $\phi[t/v]$ is just ϕ with all free (and only free) occurrences of v replaced with t.

An application of the rule looks like this:

$$
\begin{array}{cc}
& [\phi[t/v]] \\
\vdots & \vdots \\
\exists v\, \phi & \psi \\
\hline
\multicolumn{2}{c}{\psi} \quad \text{∃Elim}
\end{array}
$$

provided the constant t does not occur in $\exists v\, \phi$, or in ψ, or in any undischarged assumption other than $\phi[t/v]$ in the proof of ψ.

In practice, ∃Elim is applied in the following way: Assume that one has proved $\exists v\, \phi$. Then one picks a constant that has not been used yet and that does not occur in any premisses one has, and assumes $\phi[t/v]$. Once one has proved a sentence ψ not containing t, all assumptions of $\phi[t/v]$ are discharged and one writes ψ under the proof of $\exists v\, \phi$ and the proof of ψ. Here I have recommended using a constant t that is completely 'new' to the proof; this is not really necessary or forced by the rule, but by using a new constant one can make sure that the conditions on t in the rule are satisfied. Also, by using a constant that is not new one does not gain anything.

This rule concludes the description of the system of Natural Deduction. A list of all the rules may be found in the Appendix.

I will give some examples of proofs in which the quantifier rules are used.

EXAMPLE 6.13. $\forall x \, \neg Px \vdash \neg \exists x \, Px$.

Proof. First one assumes $\forall x \, \neg Px$ and applies $\forall$Elim:

$$\frac{\forall x \, \neg Px}{\neg Pa} \, \forall\text{Elim}$$

In order to be able to apply $\exists$Elim, one assumes Pa and continues with $\neg$Intro:

$$\cfrac{Pa \qquad \cfrac{[\forall x \, \neg Px]}{\neg Pa} \, \forall\text{Elim}}{\neg \forall x \, \neg Px} \, \neg\text{Intro}$$

With the additional assumption $\exists x \, Px$ one can apply $\exists$Elim and discharge Pa:

$$\cfrac{\exists x \, Px \qquad \cfrac{[Pa] \qquad \cfrac{[\forall x \, \neg Px]}{\neg Pa} \, \forall\text{Elim}}{\neg \forall x \, \neg Px} \, \neg\text{Intro}}{\neg \forall x \, \neg Px} \, \exists\text{Elim}$$

Now $\forall x \, \neg Px$ is assumed again to produce a contradiction that allows one to apply $\neg$Intro:

$$\cfrac{\forall x \, \neg Px \qquad \cfrac{[\exists x \, Px] \qquad \cfrac{[Pa] \qquad \cfrac{[\forall x \, \neg Px]}{\neg Pa} \, \forall\text{Elim}}{\neg \forall x \, \neg Px} \, \neg\text{Intro}}{\neg \forall x \, \neg Px} \, \exists\text{Elim}}{\neg \exists x \, Px} \, \neg\text{Intro}$$

$\exists x\, Px$ can be discharged according to ¬Intro. The only assumption that is not discharged is the leftmost occurrence of $\forall x\, \neg Px$, which is the premiss. $\square$

The next example is the converse of the previous one.

EXAMPLE 6.14. $\neg\exists x\, Px \vdash \forall x\, \neg Px$.

Proof. The conclusion $\forall x\, \neg Px$, which is to be derived, can be obtained by $\forall$Intro from $\neg Pa$. This in its turn can be obtained by ¬Intro. So Pa is assumed and $\exists$Intro is applied:

$$\frac{Pa}{\exists x\, Px}\ \exists\text{Intro}$$

Now the assumption $\neg\exists x\, Px$ is added and ¬Intro is applied:

$$\frac{\neg\exists x\, Px \qquad \dfrac{[Pa]}{\exists x\, Px}\ \exists\text{Intro}}{\neg Pa}\ \neg\text{Intro}$$

Because Pa is now discharged, $\forall$Intro can be applied:

$$\frac{\dfrac{\neg\exists x\, Px \qquad \dfrac{[Pa]}{\exists x\, Px}\ \exists\text{Intro}}{\neg Pa}\ \neg\text{Intro}}{\forall x\, \neg Px}\ \forall\text{Intro}$$

All assumptions with exception of the premiss are discharged. $\square$

In the following example, $\exists$Intro is applied in a cunning way.

EXAMPLE 6.15. $\forall x\, Rxx \vdash \forall y\, \exists z\, Ryz$.

Proof.

$$\frac{\dfrac{\dfrac{\dfrac{\forall x\, Rxx}{Raa}\ \forall\text{Elim}}{\exists z\, Raz}\ \exists\text{Intro}}{\forall y\, \exists z\, Ryz}\ \forall\text{Intro}}$$

The application of ∃Intro is legitimate: nothing in the formulation of the rule forces one to replace all occurrences of a by the variable z. The formula Raz is a formula with only one variable occurring freely; thus $\phi[t/v]$ is $Raz[a/z]$, which is the formula Raa. $\exists v\, \phi$ is then $\exists z\, Raz$. □

In Example 5.10 on page 112, I refuted $\forall x\, \exists y\, Rxy \vDash \exists y\, \forall x\, Rxy$ by means of a counterexample. Now I can establish the converse direction $\exists y\, \forall x\, Rxy \vdash \forall x\, \exists y\, Rxy$.

EXAMPLE 6.16. $\exists y\, \forall x\, Rxy \vdash \forall x\, \exists y\, Rxy$.

Proof.

$$\cfrac{\exists y\, \forall x\, Rxy \qquad \cfrac{\cfrac{\cfrac{[\forall x\, Rxb]}{Rab}\;\forall\text{Elim}}{\exists y\, Ray}\;\exists\text{Intro}}{\exists y\, Ray}\;\exists\text{Elim}}{\cfrac{\exists y\, Ray}{\forall x\, \exists y\, Rxy}\;\forall\text{Intro}}$$

The assumption $\forall x\, Rxb$ has been discharged in the penultimate step by applying ∃Elim.   □

7 Formalization in Predicate Logic

In this chapter I shall bring three strands together: the semantics of the language $\mathcal{L}_2$ of predicate logic, the system of Natural Deduction, and arguments in English. First I will turn to the relation between the semantics of $\mathcal{L}_2$ and proofs in Natural Deduction.

7.1 ADEQUACY

The rules of Natural Deduction have been chosen so as to guarantee that, if a sentence is provable (with no undischarged premises), it is logically true; and if a sentence is provable from certain premises, the corresponding argument is valid. This way, formal proofs allow one to establish that certain arguments in $\mathcal{L}_2$ are valid (and that certain sentences are logically true). In the following lemma, it is assumed that ϕ and all elements of Γ are sentences of $\mathcal{L}_2$.

LEMMA 7.1 (SOUNDNESS). *If $\Gamma \vdash \phi$, then $\Gamma \vDash \phi$.*

I will not give a proof of this claim here, but I have tried to present the rules of Natural Deduction in such a way that their soundness ought to be plausible, if not obvious.

While the soundness of the rules of Natural Deduction is fairly plausible, it is much harder to see whether one can actually prove ϕ from premises in Γ whenever $\Gamma \vDash \phi$, and whether one can prove all logical truths of $\mathcal{L}_2$. In fact, the rules of Natural Deduction are sufficient for this purpose:

THEOREM 7.2 (COMPLETENESS). *If $\Gamma \vDash \phi$, then $\Gamma \vdash \phi$.*

As before, ϕ and all elements of Γ are $\mathcal{L}_2$-sentences here.

The fact that the proof system of Natural Deduction is sound and complete is often expressed by saying that it is adequate for the semantics introduced in Chapter 5. More formally, this can be expressed in the following way:

THEOREM 7.3 (ADEQUACY). *Assume that ϕ and all elements of Γ are $\mathcal{L}_2$-sentences. Then $\Gamma \vdash \phi$ if and only if $\Gamma \vDash \phi$.*

Thus, $\vDash$ and $\vdash$ coincide even though they have been defined in completely different terms. I have defined $\vDash$ in semantic terms, that is, in terms of $\mathcal{L}_2$-structures, while $\vdash$ has been defined in purely syntactic terms, that is, in terms of rules for manipulating sentences of $\mathcal{L}_2$.

For the special case where Γ is empty, the Adequacy Theorem 7.3 means that ϕ is logically true if and only if ϕ is provable (with all assumptions discharged). This can be expressed more formally in the following way:

$$\vdash \phi \text{ if and only if } \vDash \phi$$

In practice, if one wants to show that ϕ follows from sentences in Γ, that is, if one wants to show that $\Gamma \vDash \phi$, one will usually try to construct a proof in the system of Natural Deduction because this is in most cases easier than a proof directly establishing that ϕ is true in all $\mathcal{L}_2$-structures in which all sentences in Γ are also true.

In contrast, if one wants to prove that ϕ does not follow from Γ, that is, that $\Gamma \vDash \phi$ is not the case, or $\Gamma \nvDash \phi$ for short, one will usually be better off constructing a counterexample, that is, an $\mathcal{L}_2$-structure in which all sentences of Γ are true and ϕ is not true. This is usually easier than showing that there is no proof of ϕ with sentences from Γ as the only undischarged assumptions.

In Section 5.3 I defined further semantic properties of sentences of $\mathcal{L}_2$. These properties can be defined also in terms of provability. Then the Adequacy Theorem 7.3 can be used to show that the syntactic definitions (in terms of provability) and the semantic definitions (in terms of $\mathcal{L}_2$-structures) coincide. Here consistency will serve as an example. First, consistency is defined in terms of proofs:

DEFINITION 7.4 (SYNTACTIC CONSISTENCY). *A set Γ of $\mathcal{L}_2$-sentences is syntactically consistent if and only if there is a sentence ϕ such that $\Gamma \nvdash \phi$.*

Here $\Gamma \nvdash \phi$ means that it is not the case that $\Gamma \vdash \phi$. Therefore, a set Γ of sentences is syntactically consistent if and only if it is not the case that any sentence whatsoever can be proved from premisses in Γ (as non-discharged assumptions).

Inconsistency is the opposite of consistency: a set of sentences is syntactically inconsistent if and only if it is not syntactically consistent. Thus, a set Γ of sentences is inconsistent if and only if from premisses in Γ every $\mathcal{L}_2$-sentence can be proved. That is, Γ is inconsistent if and only if $\Gamma \vdash \phi$ for every $\mathcal{L}_2$-sentence ϕ.

According to Definition 5.7, a set Γ of $\mathcal{L}_2$-sentences is semantically consistent if and only if there is an $\mathcal{L}_2$-structure $\mathcal{A}$ in which all sentences in Γ are true. Now the Adequacy Theorem can be used to show that semantic and syntactic consistency coincide:

THEOREM 7.5. *A set Γ of $\mathcal{L}_2$-sentences is semantically consistent if and only if Γ is syntactically consistent.*

Proof. Assume that the set Γ is semantically consistent. Then by Definition 5.7(iv) there is an $\mathcal{L}_2$-structure $\mathcal{A}$ in which all sentences in Γ are true. Choose a sentence ϕ which is false in that structure. Then $\Gamma \nvDash \phi$, and by the Soundness Lemma 7.1, $\Gamma \nvdash \phi$. So Γ is syntactically consistent.

To see the converse, assume that Γ is not semantically consistent. Then there is no $\mathcal{L}_2$-structure $\mathcal{A}$ in which all sentences in Γ are true. Consequently, any sentence ϕ will be true in all $\mathcal{L}_2$-structures in which all sentences of Γ are true (because there are no such structures). So $\Gamma \vDash \phi$ for all sentences ϕ of $\mathcal{L}_2$, and by Theorem 7.2, $\Gamma \vdash \phi$ for all sentences ϕ. So there is no sentence ϕ that is not provable from premisses in Γ, and, therefore, Γ is not syntactically consistent. $\qquad\square$

So far all the premiss sets used in examples have contained only a few simple sentences. A premiss set, however, may also be very complicated. For example, a premiss set could contain all of the sentences a certain person believes, or the axioms of some theory in philosophy or mathematics or medicine or any other area. A theory here is nothing more than a premiss set, that is, a set of sentences. Some theories can be logically very powerful. For instance, all of mathematics (with some possible minor exceptions) can be developed in set theory, and the axioms of set theory can be written down as $\mathcal{L}_2$-sentences.

When considering a theory, one would like to know whether it is (syntactically or semantically) consistent. Theorem 7.5 shows why consistency is such an important property of a theory: if a theory is inconsistent, anything can be proved from it. Thus, in order to show that a set of sentences is not useless as a theory (because anything can be proved from it), one has to show that the set is consistent. This can be achieved by establishing that there is an $\mathcal{L}_2$-structure in which all the sentences of the theory are true. In that case the set is semantically consistent, and by Theorem 7.5 also syntactically consistent. The tools of logic have often been used to show that theories are consistent.

These tools can be used to prove not only that theories are consistent and that sentences follow logically from certain premisses; they can also be used to investigate much more general problems about consistency, validity, and so on. I will sketch some general results of this kind here.

It would be convenient to have a general method for determining whether an arbitrary argument is valid or whether a given sentence is logically true.

If ϕ is a sentence of the language $\mathcal{L}_1$ of propositional logic, there is a method for deciding whether ϕ is logically true or not: one can use the truth-table method. In propositional logic, one can also use the truth-table method to decide whether an argument with finitely many premisses is valid or not.

The situation with $\mathcal{L}_2$ is different: one can use the system of Natural Deduction to show that a sentence is logically true, but it cannot be used to prove that a sentence is not logically true. If one does not hit upon a proof in a reasonable amount of time, this does not mean that there is no proof at all; one could simply have not yet found the proof: The maximal possible length of a proof cannot be read off from the sentence. So the system of Natural Deduction does not deliver a systematic method for deciding whether a sentence is logically true.

Church (1936) showed, using Kurt Gödel's famous Incompleteness Theorems, that there cannot be a procedure for deciding whether a sentence of $\mathcal{L}_2$ is logically true. In particular, no computer program can, given an arbitrary sentence as input, tell one infallibly whether the sentence is logically true or not, or whether a given sentence can be proved from sentences in a given theory. This holds even if there are no restrictions imposed on the computing time, computer memory, and so on. Church's result shows that, given certain sentences as input, the program will keep on calculating forever (or return an incorrect result). The precise formulation of this result is beyond the scope of this text, but it explains why the system of Natural Deduction (or any other system for predicate logic) cannot be transformed into a method that, like the truth-table method for $\mathcal{L}_1$, takes a sentence of $\mathcal{L}_2$ as input and then returns in any case after finitely many steps an answer to the question of whether the sentence is logically true or not.

Church's result also shows that there are no simple checks for the consistency of a set of assumptions: there is no systematic method – a method that could be implemented on a computer – for deciding whether a given finite set of sentences is consistent or not. Of course, one may try to find an $\mathcal{L}_2$-structure in which all sentences in the set are true, but there is again no systematic method that tells one whether there is such an $\mathcal{L}_2$-structure. Thus, proving the consistency of sets of sentences of $\mathcal{L}_2$ is a highly non-trivial affair.

7.2 AMBIGUITY

As I said at the beginning of the chapter, I want to bring together three strands: the semantics of $\mathcal{L}_2$, the system of Natural Deduction, and arguments in English. The relation between the former two has now been clarified by Theorem 7.3: the semantics of $\mathcal{L}_2$ and the proof system of Natural Deduction match up, that is, $\vDash$ and $\vdash$ coincide. Now I will turn to natural language and how to compare arguments in English to those in $\mathcal{L}_2$.

The connection between arguments in English and in $\mathcal{L}_2$ is established by translating between the two languages. So I will turn now to such translations.

In Section 4.5 I provided a sketch of how to go about translating from English into the language $\mathcal{L}_2$. In the first step the English sentence is brought into a regimented form: its logical form. In the second step the standard connectives are replaced by the respective symbols: 'there is at least one x' is replaced by $\exists x$, 'for all x' is replaced by $\forall x$, names are replaced by constants, predicate expressions are replaced by predicate letters, and so on. Most difficulties occur in the first step, while in the second step English expressions are merely mechanically replaced by corresponding symbols.

Some difficulties arise from a discrepancy between predicate expressions in English and the predicate letters of $\mathcal{L}_2$: in English the number of designators a predicate takes can vary from sentence to sentence. The following English sentences are all well formed:

> In his garage the engineer is loosening the nut with the wrench.
> The engineer is loosening the nut with the wrench.
> The engineer is loosening the nut.

In the first sentence one would like to formalize the predicate 'is loosening' as a 4-place predicate letter, in the second as a ternary predicate letter, and in the last sentence as a binary predicate letter. The language $\mathcal{L}_2$, however, does not have predicate letters with a variable number of places. If an argument contains two of the sentences above one would like to formalize the predicate 'is loosening' as the same predicate letter in both sentences, and there are some tricks that can help. For instance, one might try to reformulate the second sentence as 'In some place the engineer is loosening the nut with the wrench', thereby making it amenable to formalization by a 4-place predicate letter; then 'is loosening' can be formalized by this 4-place predicate letter in the first and second sentence. The strategy, however, does not easily generalize, and philosophers and logicians have proposed other strategies to solve the problem of variable arity. The discussion of these proposals, however, goes beyond the scope of this text.

The problem of variable arity does not arise from an ambiguity in English; rather it highlights differences in the grammars of English and $\mathcal{L}_2$. As I have already mentioned in Section 3.4, certain ambiguities can lead to two different formalizations in propositional logic. In particular, I have discussed ambiguities concerning the scope of connectives. Of course, a sentence displaying such an ambiguity has different formalizations also in $\mathcal{L}_2$ because the connectives work in $\mathcal{L}_2$ in the same way as in $\mathcal{L}_1$.

I will now discuss some other kinds of ambiguities and how to deal with them in formalizations, beginning with lexical ambiguities. The word 'bank', for instance, is lexically ambiguous. It can mean the edge of a river or a financial institution. One can analyse lexical ambiguities by formalizing 'is a bank' as two different unary predicate letters, where one predicate letter stands for '... is a bank (financial institution)' and the other for '... is a (river) bank'. Thus, a sentence containing lexically ambiguous vocabulary may have two different formalizations that are not logically equivalent.

More interestingly, there are also ambiguities that can be analysed in predicate logic by using two different sentences that do not only disagree in their predicate letters of constants but also in their structures. Usually, the indefinite article 'a' indicates existential quantification, as, for instance, in the following sentences:

> Every student owns a computer.
> A house has been damaged by a meteorite.

In some cases, however, the indefinite article is used to make a general statement that must be formalized by a universal quantifier. The following sentences are most naturally understood as general claims that are to be formalized by sentences with a universal quantifier:

A politician will never admit that he has made a mistake.
An electron is negatively charged.

Occasionally, the indefinite article is ambiguous. Often one reading will be more plausible given the context of the sentence, but sometimes it may be very hard to reach a decision about the appropriate reading. For instance, it may be difficult to decide in which way the following sentence should be understood:

A Labour MP will not agree to this proposal.

The sentence could be taken to express that at least one Labour MP will not agree or as expressing that, in general, no Labour MP will agree. Of course, such ambiguities can be made explicit with formalizations. The two readings yield the following two (respective) formalizations:

$$\exists x \, (Px \land \neg Qxa)$$
$$\forall x \, (Px \to \neg Qxa)$$

I have used the following dictionary in this formalization:

P:　　… is a Labour MP
Q:　　… agrees to …
a:　　this proposal

In the next example the indefinite article expresses existential quantification without ambiguity, but the sentence is ambiguous for another reason:

A mistake was made by every student.

In a first attempt to parse the sentence one could start as follows:

There is at least one x (x is a mistake and (every student made x))

Of course one would then go on and analyse 'every student made x' as 'for all y (if (y is a student), then (y made x))'. According to this analysis, there is at least one mistake that was made by every student; so every student made the same mistake (and possibly more). On this reading the logical form would be as follows:

> There is at least one x ((x is a mistake) and for all y (if (y is a student), then (y made x)))

Using the dictionary below, this yields the following $\mathcal{L}_2$-sentence:

$$\exists x\, (Qx \wedge \forall y\, (Py \to Ryx)) \tag{7.1}$$

> P: ... is a student
> Q: ... is a mistake
> R: ... made ...

There is, however, an alternative reading. The original sentence may be taken to say what would be more naturally expressed by the following sentence:

> Every student made a mistake,

where it is understood that it could well be the case that each student made different mistakes, and there is no one mistake that was made by all students. This reading results in the following logical form:

> For all y (if (y is a student), then there is at least one x ((x is a mistake) and (y made x)))

The formalization is obviously different from (7.1):

$$\forall y\, (Py \to \exists x\, (Qx \wedge Ryx)) \tag{7.2}$$

Without additional information, one cannot decide which of the two readings is the correct one. The original sentence is ambiguous.

This kind of ambiguity is akin to the scope ambiguities in propositional logic discussed on page 65. There the 'grouping' of connectives was not uniquely determined by the original English sentence, which resulted in two different formalizations, $P \wedge (Q \vee R)$ and $(P \wedge Q) \vee R$. In that example it was not clear whether $\vee$ should be in the scope of $\wedge$ (as in the first sentence) or $\wedge$ should be in the scope of $\vee$. In the present case, on the first reading (7.1), the existential quantifier comes first so that the universal quantifier 'falls under' the existential one, while the order is reversed in the second formalization (7.2).

The definition of the scope of (an occurrence of) a quantifier is similar to the definition of the scope of a connective on page 65. Simultaneously I also define the scope of a connective in an $\mathcal{L}_2$-formula; it's the same definition as for $\mathcal{L}_1$ except that I consider now subformulae rather than subsentences.

DEFINITION 7.6 (SCOPE OF A QUANTIFIER OR CONNECTIVE IN $\mathcal{L}_2$). *The scope of an occurrence of a quantifier or a connective in a sentence ϕ of $\mathcal{L}_2$ is the occurrence of the smallest $\mathcal{L}_2$-formula that contains that occurrence of the quantifier or connective and is part of ϕ.*

Thus, in (7.1) the entire sentence, including the occurrence of $\forall y$, is the scope of (the single occurrence of) the existential quantifier. The scope of the occurrence of the universal quantifier $\forall y$ is the underbraced part:

$$\exists x (Qx \wedge \underbrace{\forall y (Py \to Ryx})})$$
$$\text{scope of } \forall y$$

So the above ambiguity is another case of scope ambiguity because the original sentence 'Every student made a mistake' leaves it open whether the universal quantifier is in the scope of the existential quantifier or vice versa.

7.3 EXTENSIONALITY

If the constants a and b have the same extension in an $\mathcal{L}_2$-structure $\mathcal{A}$, that is, if a and b denote the same object, then replacing a by b in a true sentence will yield a true sentence. For instance, if a and b both denote Rome in some $\mathcal{L}_2$-structure $\mathcal{A}$, that is, if $|a|_{\mathcal{A}}$ and $|b|_{\mathcal{A}}$ are both Rome, then, for example, Pa will be true if and only if Pb is true. This is easily seen from Definition 5.2 of satisfaction: assume Pa is true, that is, $|Pa|_{\mathcal{A}} = T$ and reason as follows:

$|Pa|_{\mathcal{A}} = T$	assumption
$|a|_{\mathcal{A}} \in |P|_{\mathcal{A}}$	Definition 5.2(i)
$|b|_{\mathcal{A}} \in |P|_{\mathcal{A}}$	by assumption $|a|_{\mathcal{A}} = |b|_{\mathcal{A}}$
$|Pb|_{\mathcal{A}} = T$	Definition 5.2(i)

In the third line I used the assumption that a and b have the same extension, that is, that $|a|_{\mathcal{A}} = |b|_{\mathcal{A}}$. This shows that if Pa is true in $\mathcal{A}$, so is Pb.

The argument generalizes to more complex sentences: as long as a and b have the same extension, they can be replaced in any sentence by one another without changing the truth-value of that sentence.

If constants, sentence letters, and predicate letters are replaced in an $\mathcal{L}_2$-sentence by other constants, sentence letters, and predicate letters (respectively) that have the same extension in a given $\mathcal{L}_2$-structure, then the truth-value of the sentence in that $\mathcal{L}_2$-structure does not change.

I will not prove the general claim that all sentence letters, predicate letters, and constants with the same extensions respectively can be substituted 'salva veritate' (Latin shorthand for 'without making a true sentence false'), but the above example of the sentence Pa should make the general claim plausible. Languages in which these substitutions are possible are called 'extensional': in extensional languages a sentence's truth-value depends only on the semantic values of the non-logical symbols, that is, on the extensions of the names, on the relations that are the extensions of predicate expressions, and so on.

In English it is often possible to substitute designators denoting the same object for one another *salva veritate*, that is, without affecting the truth-value of the sentence. For instance, the designator 'Qomolangma' is just the official Tibetan name for Mount Everest. Thus 'Qomolangma' and 'Mount Everest' denote the same mountain. So if the sentence

Mount Everest is 8 850 metres high

is true, then

Qomolangma is 8 850 metres high

must be true. Clearly whether I use 'Mount Everest' or 'Qomolangma' to denote the highest mountain, the truth-value of the sentence will be the same. I could even replace 'Mount Everest' by the description 'the mountain Edmund Hillary climbed on 29 May 1953' without affecting the sentence's truth-value:

The mountain Edmund Hillary climbed on 29 May 1953 is 8 850 metres high.

So here English behaves very much like $\mathcal{L}_2$: I can replace designators designating the same object by one another without changing the truth-value of this sentence in the same way I have been able to substitute b for a in the sentence Pa without changing its truth-value in $\mathcal{A}$ (assuming that $|a|_{\mathcal{A}} = |b|_{\mathcal{A}}$).

English, however, is not extensional. There are also sentences such that substituting designators denoting the same object can change their truth-value.

Assume that the following sentence is true:

Tom believes that Mount Everest is 8 850 metres high.

If Tom does not believe that Qomolangma is Mount Everest if he believes, for instance, that it is a small mountain in the Alps, then the following sentence is presumably false:

Tom believes that Qomolangma is 8 850 metres high.

And the sentence

Tom believes that the mountain Edmund Hillary climbed on 29 May 1953 is 8 850 metres high might also be false, although 'Mount Everest', 'Qomolangma', and 'the mountain Edmund Hillary climbed on 29 May 1953' all denote the same object. Tom might have no idea whether Hillary climbed a mountain on 29 May 1953 and, if so, which mountain Hillary climbed on that day. This example shows that English is not an extensional language.

A similar point can be made about predicate expressions. Assuming again that the animals with kidneys are exactly the animals with hearts, the following substitution may transform the true first sentence into a false sentence:[1]

> Tom believes that all snails have hearts.
> Tom believes that all snails have kidneys.

Tom might believe that all snails have hearts, but he might not have a view on whether they also have kidneys. He may even believe that they lack kidneys.

Another example of the failure of extensionality is the following pair of sentences:

> It is logically true that all animals with hearts have hearts.
> It is logically true that all animals with hearts have kidneys.

The first sentence is true, while the second is false: it is not logically true that all animals with hearts have kidneys.

In the above examples, 'that'-sentences have been used to produce counterexamples to the extensionality of English. The problematic substitutions were made after such phrases as 'Tom believes that' or 'It is logically true that'. There are also cases of simpler sentences, without 'that', where extensionality fails:

> Oedipus is looking for his mother.

This sentence may well be true since Oedipus was abandoned as a baby. Now he is married to and lives with Jocasta who, unbeknownst to him, is his mother. So the following sentence might be false at the same time:

---

1 The qualifications from page 5 footnote 2 apply.

Oedipus is looking for Jocasta.

She might actually be sitting right next to him. Since 'Jocasta' and 'Oedipus' mother' denote the same person, the example provides another case of the failure of extensionality.

The failure of extensionality of English imposes certain restrictions on the formalizations of English sentences in the language of predicate logic. In the above example, one might be tempted to formalize

Oedipus is looking for Jocasta

as P^2ab with the following dictionary:

P^2:   ... is looking for ...
  a: Oedipus
  b: Jocasta

This translation is not correct: '... is looking for ...' does not express a relation, that is, a set of ordered pairs. If it did, it would express the set (relation) of all pairs $\langle d, e \rangle$ such that d is looking for e; and if the pair ⟨Oedipus, Oedipus' mother⟩ is in that set, then ⟨Oedipus, Jocasta⟩ is necessarily also in that set since it is the same ordered pair: ordered pairs are identical if they agree in their first and second components, and Oedipus' mother and Jocasta are the same object. So it would be true that Oedipus is looking for Jocasta, which is not the case. Thus, '... is looking for ...' cannot be formalized as a binary predicate letter, because this is assigned a binary relation as its extension in any $\mathcal{L}_2$-structure.

However, one can still formalize '... is looking for Oedipus' mother' by a unary predicate letter. The English predicate expression '... is looking for Oedipus' mother' does express a unary relation, that is, a set: the designator 'Oedipus' may be replaced by any other designator for Oedipus without changing the truth-value of the sentence. In any case, whenever one has a designator t such that 't is looking for Oedipus' mother' is true and some designator s refers to the same object as t, the sentence 's is looking for Oedipus' mother' is true as well.

By a similar argument one can show that the predicate expression '... believes that ... is high' must not be formalized as a binary predicate letter. This can be done by considering the following example again:

Tom believes that Mount Everest is high.

The formalization by the sentence $R^2 a_1 b_1$ with the following dictionary is not correct:

R^2: ... believes that ... is high

a_1: Tom

b_1: Mount Everest

Assume that '...believes that ...is high' is formalized as a binary predicate letter; then the following problem arises: If $\mathcal{B}$ is an $\mathcal{L}_2$-structure and the pair ⟨Tom, Mount Everest⟩ is an element of the semantic value of R^2, that is, of the relation $|R^2|_\mathcal{B}$, then ⟨Tom, Qomolangma⟩ is by necessity also an element of that relation. This is due to the fact that ⟨Tom, Mount Everest⟩ and ⟨Tom, Qomolangma⟩ are the same ordered pair with Tom as first component and the highest mountain on earth as the second. But the sentence

Tom believes that Qomolangma is high

may be false. So '... believes that ... is high' cannot be formalized as a binary predicate letter.

The best formalization with the tools available might be $Q^1 a$, where Q^1 is translated as '... believes that Mount Everest is high'.

Only if an English predicate expresses a relation, can it be adequately formalized as a predicate letter.

This also includes unary predicate letters, which denote unary relations, that is, sets (see the end of Section 1.4).

7.4 PREDICATE LOGIC AND ARGUMENTS IN ENGLISH

Many remarks about, and definitions of, formalizations carry over from propositional logic to predicate logic. In particular, Definition 3.5 can be reformulated for predicate logic in the obvious way:

DEFINITION 7.7.

(i) *An English sentence is logically true in predicate logic if and only if its formalization in predicate logic is logically true.*

(ii) *An English sentence is a contradiction in predicate logic if and only if its formalization in predicate logic is a contradiction.*

(iii) *A set of English sentences is consistent in predicate logic if and only if the set of their formalizations in predicate logic is semantically consistent.*[2]

Similarly, the definition of validity of English arguments in predicate logic is analogous to Definition 3.6:

DEFINITION 7.8. *An argument in English is valid in predicate logic if and only if its formalization in the language $\mathcal{L}_2$ of predicate logic is valid.*

Of course, an argument in English is valid if it is valid in predicate logic, that is, if its formalization in $\mathcal{L}_2$ is valid. So an argument in English is valid, if its formalization in $\mathcal{L}_2$ is a valid argument. However, on the view of many logicians, there are valid arguments in English that are not valid in predicate logic. I will return to the question whether there are such English arguments later.

As in the case of propositional logic, talking about the formalization of a sentence in $\mathcal{L}_2$ is not unproblematic since there may be more than one formalization (see Chapter 3): if a sentence is ambiguous and has two or more formalizations, the sentence may be logically true in predicate logic on one reading, but not on another.

To illustrate how the methods of predicate logic can be used to analyse arguments in English, I will now go through some examples, starting with a simple and famous example:

> All men are mortal. Socrates is a man. Therefore, Socrates is mortal.

---

2 I could have used the notion of syntactic consistency here instead as any set of sentences is semantically consistent iff it is syntactically consistent by Theorem 7.5.

Clearly, the argument is valid. In order to establish its validity formally, I will formalize the premises as $\forall x(Px \to Qx)$ and Pc and the conclusion as Qc with the following dictionary:

P: … is a man
Q: … is mortal
c: Socrates

The resulting argument in $\mathcal{L}_2$ is valid:

EXAMPLE 7.9. $\forall x(Px \to Qx), Pc \vdash Qc$.

Proof. A proof in Natural Deduction looks like this:

$$\cfrac{Pc \qquad \cfrac{\forall x(Px \to Qx)}{Pc \to Qc}\ \forall\,\text{Elim}}{Qc}\ {\to}\text{Elim}$$

□

The formalization and the proof show that the English argument is valid in predicate logic and, thus, formally valid.

Next, I will turn to an example that was analysed on page 69 in the chapter on propositional logic:

Unless Alfred is an eminent logician, it is not the case that both Kurt and Alfred are eminent logicians.

The sentence has the formalization

$$Pa \vee \neg(Pa \wedge Pb)$$

with the following dictionary:

P: … is an eminent logician
a: Alfred
b: Kurt

The claim $\vdash Pa \vee \neg(Pa \wedge Pb)$ can be established by the following proof:

$$\cfrac{\cfrac{\cfrac{\cfrac{[\neg(Pa \land Pb)]}{Pa \lor \neg(Pa \land Pb)} \quad \cfrac{[\neg(Pa \lor \neg(Pa \land Pb))]}{Pa \land Pb} \neg\text{Elim}}{Pa}\text{vIntro1}}{Pa \lor \neg(Pa \land Pb)} \quad [\neg(Pa \lor \neg(Pa \land Pb))]}{Pa \lor \neg(Pa \land Pb)}\neg\text{Elim}$$

Hence, the English sentence is logically true in predicate logic. An inspection of the proof shows that I have only used rules from propositional logic: the formalization of the designator 'Alfred' as a constant and of '… is an eminent logician' as a predicate letter has not been used at all. The parsing of the sentence 'Alfred is an eminent logician' into a predicate expression and a designator is not really needed in order to see that the sentence is logically true: if I had formalized the sentences 'Alfred is an eminent logician' and 'Kurt is an eminent logician' just with two sentence letters, I would also have obtained a logically true $\mathcal{L}_2$-sentence (which is also a tautology). In fact, on page 70 I already showed that the sentence is logically true in propositional logic, that is, it is a tautology. Thus, I did not need to use the more detailed formalization in order to establish that the English sentence is a tautology. This observation can be generalized:

If a partial formalization of an English sentence is logically true, then that English sentence is logically true in predicate logic. Similarly, if a partial formalization of an English argument is valid, then that English argument is valid in predicate logic.

By a partial formalization of a sentence I mean here a translation of that sentence into the formal language ($\mathcal{L}_1$ or $\mathcal{L}_2$) that has been obtained according to the rules for translating, but that has not reached its full formalization. Thus, in order to show that an argument is valid, one does not always have to give a full formalization. Of course it is not wrong to give the full formalization, but giving merely a partial formalization will be less laborious.

I will illustrate this point with the following argument:

> Every student has a computer. Wilma doesn't have a computer. Therefore Wilma isn't a student.

I have already formalized the first premiss on page 91. This time I will formalize the expression 'has a computer' as a unary predicate letter, that is, I will not formalize the existential quantifier contained in '... has a computer' as on page 91.

P: ... is a student
P_1:   ... has a computer
a: Wilma

With this dictionary the formalization of the first premiss is $\forall x (Px \rightarrow P_1 x)$, the formalization of the second premiss is $\neg P_1 a$, and the formalization of the conclusion is $\neg Pa$. This yields a valid argument in predicate logic: $\forall x (Px \rightarrow P_1 x), \neg P_1 a \vdash \neg Pa$ (see Exercise 6.3(i)). Thus, the English argument is valid in predicate logic. This has been established without giving the full formalization of the first premiss as on page 91, that is, $\forall x (Px \rightarrow \exists y (Rxy \wedge Qy))$.

The next argument (or at least a similar one) has played a role in the development of logic.[3]

(H) Horses are animals. Therefore every head of a horse is the head of an animal.

Here is the logical form of the premiss:

for all x: (if (x is a horse) then (x is an animal))

Thus the premiss can be formalized as $\forall x (Px \rightarrow Qx)$.

The logical form of the conclusion of (H) is more difficult to determine. The first step should be clear, however:

---

3 The dominating form of logic since antiquity was Aristotle's syllogistics. But by the 19th century some shortcomings of syllogistics had become clear. Syllogistics is not incorrect, and it is not in conflict with modern logic, but it is weaker than predicate logic. In the 19th century various logicians argued that syllogistics cannot cope with arguments of certain types. An argument similar to the one above was used by De Morgan (1847, pages 114–115) to demonstrate the insufficiency of syllogistics because its validity cannot be shown in syllogistic logic.

for all x (if x is the head of a horse then x is the head of an animal)

The expression 'x is the head of a horse' need not be further analysed for showing the validity of the argument. The following logical form of the conclusion will suffice:

for all x (if there is a y: ((y is a horse) and (x is the head of y)) then there is a y: ((y is an animal) and (x is the head of y)))

Thus, the conclusion can be formalized as the following $\mathcal{L}_2$-sentence:

$$\forall x(\exists y(Py \wedge Rxy) \rightarrow \exists y(Qy \wedge Rxy))$$

I have used the following dictionary:

   P: ... is a horse
   Q: ... is an animal
   R: ... is the head of ...

The resulting $\mathcal{L}_2$-argument is valid:

EXAMPLE 7.10. $\forall x(Px \rightarrow Qx) \vdash \forall x(\exists y(Py \wedge Rxy) \rightarrow \exists y(Qy \wedge Rxy))$.

Proof.

$$
\cfrac{
\cfrac{
\cfrac{\dfrac{[Pb \wedge Rab]}{Pb} \quad \dfrac{\forall x(Px \rightarrow Qx)}{Pb \rightarrow Qb}}{Qb} \quad \dfrac{[Pb \wedge Rab]}{Rab}
}{
\cfrac{\dfrac{Qb \wedge Rab}{\exists y(Qy \wedge Ray)} \text{ }^{\exists\text{Intro}}}{}
}
\quad [\exists y(Py \wedge Ray)]
}{
\cfrac{\exists y(Qy \wedge Ray)}{\cfrac{\exists y(Py \wedge Ray) \rightarrow \exists y(Qy \wedge Ray)}{\forall x(\exists y(Py \wedge Rxy) \rightarrow \exists y(Qy \wedge Rxy))} \text{ }^{\forall\text{Intro}}} \text{ }^{\rightarrow\text{Intro}}
} \text{ }^{\exists\text{Elim}}
$$

$\square$

Therefore, argument (H) is valid in predicate logic and, therefore, logically (formally) valid.

One does need to use a full formalization in order to show that the next argument is valid.

There is not a single moral person. Therefore all persons
are immoral.

If 'immoral' is understood as 'not moral', the argument can be formalized as follows:

$$\neg\exists x(Px \wedge Qx) \vdash \forall y(Py \rightarrow \neg Qy) \tag{7.3}$$

The dictionary is obvious:

  P: ... is a person
  Q: ... is moral

Claim (7.3) can be proved as follows:

$$\cfrac{\neg\exists x(Px \wedge Qx) \qquad \cfrac{\cfrac{[Pa \wedge Qa]}{\exists x(Px \wedge Qx)}\,\exists\text{Intro}}{\neg(Pa \wedge Qa)}\,\neg\text{Intro} \qquad \cfrac{[Pa] \qquad [Qa]}{Pa \wedge Qa}}{\cfrac{\cfrac{\neg Qa}{Pa \rightarrow \neg Qa}\,\rightarrow\text{Intro}}{\forall y(Py \rightarrow \neg Qy)}\,\forall\text{Intro}}$$

The arguments considered so far in this section have all been valid.
I will now consider an argument in English that is not valid:

All lottery tickets are winners or losers. Therefore all tickets are winners.

Using this trivial example I shall explain in some detail how the semantics of $\mathcal{L}_2$ can be employed to show that this argument is not valid in
predicate logic.

First I will formalize the argument. The premiss becomes

$$\forall x(Px \rightarrow Qx \vee Rx),$$

and the conclusion

$$\forall x(Px \rightarrow Qx).$$

The dictionary should be obvious:

P: ... is a lottery ticket
Q: ... is a winner
R: ... is a loser

I want to disprove the validity of the resulting $\mathcal{L}_2$-argument, that is, I want to show the following:

$$\forall x(Px \rightarrow Qx \lor Rx) \nvDash \forall x(Px \rightarrow Qx) \qquad (7.4)$$

This can be achieved by means of a counterexample, that is, by means of an $\mathcal{L}_2$-structure in which the premiss is true and the conclusion is false. The $\mathcal{L}_2$-structure $\mathcal{F}$ constitutes such a counterexample; it has a domain with only the number 1 in it:

$$D_{\mathcal{F}} = \{1\}$$
$$|P|_{\mathcal{F}} = \{1\}$$
$$|Q|_{\mathcal{F}} = \emptyset$$
$$|R|_{\mathcal{F}} = \{1\}$$

The semantic values for the other constants, sentence letters, and predicate letters do not matter, and I will not specify them.

Next, I will show that the premiss is true in $\mathcal{F}$. Over the domain $D_{\mathcal{F}}$ there is only a single variable assignment α, because there is only one object in the domain and for any variable v, $\alpha(v)$ must be 1, so $|x|_{\mathcal{F}}^{\alpha} = 1$. Now one can reason as follows:

$|x|_{\mathcal{F}}^{\alpha} \in |R|_{\mathcal{F}}$	definition of $\mathcal{F}$
$|Rx|_{\mathcal{F}}^{\alpha} = T$	Definition 5.2(i)
$|Rx \lor Qx|_{\mathcal{F}}^{\alpha} = T$	Definition 5.2(iv)
$|Px \rightarrow Rx \lor Qx|_{\mathcal{F}}^{\alpha} = T$	Definition 5.2(v)
$|\forall x(Px \rightarrow Rx \lor Qx)|_{\mathcal{F}} = T$	Definition 5.2(vii)

The last line holds because there is only one variable assignment over $D_{\mathcal{F}}$. Thus, the premiss is indeed true in the $\mathcal{L}_2$-structure $\mathcal{F}$.

It remains to show that the conclusion is false in $\mathcal{F}$:

$\|x\|^{\alpha}_{\mathcal{F}}$ is not in $\|Q\|_{\mathcal{F}}$	definition of $\mathcal{F}$
$\|Qx\|^{\alpha}_{\mathcal{F}} = F$	Definition 5.2(i)
$\|x\|^{\alpha}_{\mathcal{F}} \in \|P\|_{\mathcal{F}}$	definition of $\mathcal{F}$
$\|Px\|^{\alpha}_{\mathcal{F}} = T$	Definition 5.2(i)
$\|Px \rightarrow Qx\|^{\alpha}_{\mathcal{F}} = F$	Definition 5.2(v)
$\|\forall x(Px \rightarrow Qx)\|_{\mathcal{F}} = F$	Definition 5.2(vii)

The last line shows that the conclusion is not true in $\mathcal{F}$, and thus the claim 7.4 is established. Consequently, the English argument is not valid in predicate logic. This procedure can be applied generally:

> *In order to show that an English argument is not valid in predicate logic, one will formalize the argument and provide a counterexample to the resulting $\mathcal{L}_2$-argument.*

I have said that one can show that an English argument is valid by providing a partial formalization that is a valid $\mathcal{L}_2$-argument. In order to refute the validity of an English argument, merely partial formalizations cannot be used: usually an English argument that is valid in predicate logic will have some $\mathcal{L}_2$-formalization that is not valid. Thus, in order to show that an English argument is not valid in predicate logic, one needs to consider its full formalization.

8 Identity and Definite Descriptions

In this chapter I will introduce a third formal language. This new language $\mathcal{L}_=$ is the language of predicate logic with identity; it is only a slight refinement of the language $\mathcal{L}_2$ of predicate logic: $\mathcal{L}_=$ is just $\mathcal{L}_2$ with the addition of the new symbol = for identity.

8.1 QUALITATIVE AND NUMERICAL IDENTITY

Philosophers distinguish two different notions of identity: qualitative identity and numerical identity. In the following example I present a case of qualitative identity.

> There is a fountain pen in my teaching room and another fountain pen in my study at home. They are the same model, the same colour, and both are still in pristine condition. Thus, I have two identical fountain pens.

There are two pens, and they are qualitatively identical because they are in all relevant aspects very similar.

To explain numerical identity, I will expand the example a little bit:

> A fountain pen expert sees my pen at home after having seen the pen in my teaching room the day before. He may wonder whether I have taken the pen home and ask: 'Is this the same pen as the pen in your teaching room?' or 'Is this pen identical with the pen I saw yesterday?'

He knows all the ways that the pen at my home and the pen in my teaching room are similar, and so he is not asking whether they are the same colour or are of the same brand; rather he wants to know whether it is the same pen, that is, whether he has seen two (qualitatively identical) pens or whether he has seen one and the same pen. So in his question identity has to be understood numerically. In the numerical sense the pen in my teaching room is not identical with the pen in my study at home, that is, there are *two* pens.

Occasionally it is not clear which kind of identity is at issue in a given sentence. The claim

Robin saw the same tree years later in the garden

might be taken to express that Robin saw one and the same tree in the garden years later, or that he saw a tree of the same kind in the garden years later.

Qualitative identity may be formalized by a binary predicate letter of $\mathcal{L}_2$. Its treatment in predicate logic with identity does not differ from the treatment of most other binary predicates.

Numerical identity, in contrast, is given a special status. In what follows I shall talk exclusively about numerical identity. Numerical identity is formalized by a new, special predicate letter.

8.2 THE SYNTAX OF $\mathcal{L}_=$

All formulae of $\mathcal{L}_2$ are also formulae of $\mathcal{L}_=$. But $\mathcal{L}_=$ also includes a new kind of atomic formula.

DEFINITION 8.1 (ATOMIC FORMULAE OF $\mathcal{L}_=$). *All atomic formulae of $\mathcal{L}_2$ are atomic formulae of $\mathcal{L}_=$. Furthermore, if s and t are variables or constants, then s = t is an atomic formula of $\mathcal{L}_=$.*

Examples of atomic formulae of $\mathcal{L}_=$ are $x = x$, $x = z_{56}$, $a = y$, and $a_{34} = c_{22}$, and atomic formulae of $\mathcal{L}_2$ such as $P_5^3 x x c_3$. Otherwise, there are no deviations from the syntax of $\mathcal{L}_2$, and one can build complex formulae using connectives and quantifiers as in $\mathcal{L}_2$ in accordance with Definition 4.7 of a formula of $\mathcal{L}_2$. Of course, now one must also allow for =. The new symbol = behaves exactly like a binary predicate letter, with the exception that = is written between the variables or constants.

Writing the identity symbol like other predicate letters as the first symbol in atomic formulae would look odd, as we are used to writing $x = y$ rather than $= xy$, but that is the only reason for writing $x = y$ rather than $= xy$.

The formulae of $\mathcal{L}_=$ are defined in the same way as the formulae of $\mathcal{L}_2$ in Definition 4.7, with the only exception that the new atomic formulae can be used.

DEFINITION 8.2 (FORMULAE OF $\mathcal{L}_=$).

   (i) *All atomic formulae of $\mathcal{L}_=$ are formulae of $\mathcal{L}_=$.*
  (ii) *If ϕ and ψ are formulae of $\mathcal{L}_=$, then $\neg\phi$, $(\phi \wedge \psi)$, $(\phi \vee \psi)$, $(\phi \rightarrow \psi)$, and $(\phi \leftrightarrow \psi)$ are formulae of $\mathcal{L}_=$.*
 (iii) *If v is a variable and ϕ is a formula of $\mathcal{L}_=$ then $\forall v\, \phi$ and $\exists v\, \phi$ are formulae of $\mathcal{L}_=$.*

For instance, $\neg\, x = y$ and $\forall x\, (Rxy_2 \rightarrow y_2 = x)$ are formulae of $\mathcal{L}_=$.

All other definitions from Section 4.2 carry over as well. Sentences of $\mathcal{L}_=$ are defined as those formulae in which no variable occurs freely. Also, the bracketing conventions are the same as for $\mathcal{L}_2$.

8.3 THE SEMANTICS OF $\mathcal{L}_=$

The semantics for $\mathcal{L}_=$ is just a small variation on the semantics for $\mathcal{L}_2$, and so it is not necessary to introduce a new kind of structure: $\mathcal{L}_2$-structures are used for the semantics of $\mathcal{L}_=$.

Only Definition 5.2 needs to be amended by adding the following additional clause to (i)–(viii), where $\mathcal{A}$ is an $\mathcal{L}_2$-structure, s is a variable or constant, and t is a variable or constant:

  (ix) $|s = t|_{\mathcal{A}}^{\alpha} = \mathrm{T}$ *if and only if* $|s|_{\mathcal{A}}^{\alpha} = |t|_{\mathcal{A}}^{\alpha}$.

Thus, in the semantics for $\mathcal{L}_=$, the symbol $=$ is always interpreted as numerical identity. In (ix) the symbol $=$ is used in two different ways: its first occurrence is a symbol of the formal language $\mathcal{L}_=$; the two subsequent occurrences belong to the language we are using to describe $\mathcal{L}_=$.

In order to avoid this ambiguity some authors put a dot under the symbol of the formal language, but this convention has not really caught on. Alternatively, one could avoid the use of = outside the formal language $\mathcal{L}_=$ by reformulating (ix) in the following way:

(ix) The variable assignment α satisfies $s = t$ in $\mathcal{A}$ if and only if $|s|_{\mathcal{A}}^{\alpha}$ and $|t|_{\mathcal{A}}^{\alpha}$ are the same object.

In the following I will not try to avoid the use of = in these two different roles: it should be clear for every occurrence of the symbol whether it is used as a symbol of $\mathcal{L}_=$ or as a symbol of our everyday mathematical language.

It follows from clause (ix) that for any $\mathcal{L}_2$-structure $\mathcal{A}$, $|a = a|_{\mathcal{A}} = $ T and for any variable assignment α over $\mathcal{A}$, $|x = x|_{\mathcal{A}}^{\alpha} = $ T, because, trivially, $|x|_{\mathcal{A}}^{\alpha}$ is the same object as $|x|_{\mathcal{A}}^{\alpha}$, and $|a|_{\mathcal{A}}$ is the same object as $|a|_{\mathcal{A}}$. Of course, the same applies to variables other than x and to constants other than a.

The definitions of validity of arguments, of semantic consistency, of logically true sentences, and so on, carry over from Definitions 5.7 and 5.8.

The method of counterexamples can be applied in the same way as it was for the language $\mathcal{L}_2$. As an example I will show that $\exists x \exists y \neg x = y$ is not logically implied (in predicate logic with identity) by the premiss $\exists x \, Px \wedge \exists y \, Py$.

EXAMPLE 8.3. $\exists x \, Px \wedge \exists y \, Py \nvDash \exists x \exists y \, \neg x = y$

The argument could be a formalization of the following English argument:

> There is a painting and there is a painting. Therefore there are at least two things.

A more literal translation of the conclusion $\exists x \exists y \neg x = y$ would be 'there is a thing such that there is a thing that is not identical with the first'; but that is just a longwinded way of saying that there are at least two things.

The premiss just makes the same claim twice, namely that there is a painting. The use of the two variables x and y does not imply that there are two different paintings. This yields the idea for the following proof.

Proof. Let B be an $\mathcal{L}_2$-structure with the (painting of) Mona Lisa as the only element in its domain of discourse, and $\{$ the Mona Lisa $\}$ as the extension of P:

$$D_B = \{ \text{ the Mona Lisa } \}$$
$$|P|_B = \{ \text{ the Mona Lisa } \}$$

First I will show that the premiss is true in this structure.

There is exactly one variable assignment α over B: it assigns the Mona Lisa to all variables, so $|x|_{\mathcal{A}}^{\alpha}$ is the Mona Lisa.

the Mona Lisa $\in \{$the Mona Lisa$\}$
$|x|_B^{\alpha} \in |P|_B$
$|Px|_B^{\alpha} = \text{T}$ Definition 5.2(i)
$|\exists x\, Px|_B = \text{T}$ Definition 5.2(viii)

Since α assigns the Mona Lisa to y as well, the same reasoning can be applied to y:

$|y|_B^{\alpha} \in |P|_B$
$|Py|_B^{\alpha} = \text{T}$ Definition 5.2(i)
$|\exists y\, Py|_B = \text{T}$ Definition 5.2(viii)

Taking the last lines together, one can infer the following by Definition 5.2(iii):

$$|\exists x\, Px \wedge \exists y\, Py|_B = \text{T}$$

So the premiss is true in B, and it remains to show that the conclusion is not true in B.

Assume to the contrary that the conclusion is true in B, that is, assume that $|\exists x\, \exists y\, \neg x = y|_B = \text{T}$. Then, by Definition 5.2(viii), for at least one variable assignment the following must obtain:

$$|\exists y\, \neg x = y|_B^{\alpha} = \text{T}$$

Applying Definition 5.2(viii) again, one can conclude that there is a variable assignment β over $\mathcal{B}$, differing from α in y at most, such that the following obtains:

$$|\neg x = y|_{\mathcal{B}}^{\beta} = T$$

(In fact, there is only one variable assignment over $\mathcal{B}$ and therefore α and β are the same variable assignment, but I do not make use of this fact here.)

By Definition 5.2(ii) it follows that

$$|x = y|_{\mathcal{B}}^{\beta} = F. \tag{8.1}$$

Since there is only one object in the domain of $\mathcal{B}$, namely the Mona Lisa, $|x|_{\mathcal{B}}^{\beta}$ and $|y|_{\mathcal{B}}^{\beta}$ are the same object. Thus, $|x|_{\mathcal{B}}^{\beta} = |y|_{\mathcal{B}}^{\beta}$, which implies the following by the above special supplementary clause (ix) for Definition 5.2:

$$|x = y|_{\mathcal{B}}^{\beta} = T$$

This contradicts (8.1), which followed from the assumption that the conclusion $\exists x \, \exists y \, \neg x = y$ is true in $\mathcal{B}$. Thus, the conclusion is not true in $\mathcal{B}$, and it has been shown that $\exists x \, \exists y \, \neg x = y$ does not follow from the premiss $\exists x \, Px \wedge \exists y \, Py$. $\square$

8.4 PROOF RULES FOR IDENTITY

In order to obtain a proof system that is sound and complete with respect to the semantics for $\mathcal{L}_=$, the system of Natural Deduction needs to be expanded so as to include an introduction and an elimination rule for identity.

The introduction rule allows one to assume $a = a$ (and similarly for all other constants) and to discharge $a = a$ immediately:

> =Intro   *Any assumption of the form $t = t$ where t is a constant can and must be discharged.*

Hence, a proof with an application of =Intro looks like this:

$$\frac{[t=t]}{\vdots} \quad \text{=Intro}$$

To motivate the elimination rule I will look at the following informal way of reasoning: if one has established that Mount Everest is Qomolangma and that Mount Everest is in Asia, then one can conclude that Qomolangma is in Asia. The elimination rule for identity is the formal counterpart of the general principle legitimating this substitution. In this rule ϕ is a formula of $\mathcal{L}_=$ with at most one variable v occurring freely.

> =Elim   *If s and t are constants, the result of appending $\phi[t/v]$ to a proof of $\phi[s/v]$ and a proof of $s = t$ or $t = s$ is a proof of $\phi[t/v]$.*

The graphical representation of the rule looks as follows:

$$\frac{\begin{matrix} \vdots & & \vdots \\ \phi[s/v] & & s=t \end{matrix}}{\phi[t/v]} \text{=Elim} \qquad \frac{\begin{matrix} \vdots & & \vdots \\ \phi[s/v] & & t=s \end{matrix}}{\phi[t/v]} \text{=Elim}$$

Strictly speaking, only one of the versions is needed, as from $s = t$ one can always obtain $t = s$ using only one of the rules, as will be shown in Example 8.5. Having both versions available is, however, more convenient.

I give some examples illustrating the use of these rules.

EXAMPLE 8.4. ⊢ $\forall x\ x = x$

Proof. The proof is very short:

$$\frac{[a=a]}{\forall x\ x=x}$$

First $a = a$ is assumed and immediately discharged by =Intro. Then $\forall$Intro can be applied without violating the restriction on constants.

□

EXAMPLE 8.5. $\vdash \forall x\, \forall y\, (x=y \to y=x)$

Proof.

$$
\dfrac{\dfrac{\dfrac{\dfrac{\dfrac{[a=a] \qquad [a=b]}{b=a}\ {=}\text{Elim}}{a=b \to b=a}\ {\to}\text{Intro}}{\forall y\, (a=y \to y=a)}\ \forall\text{Intro}}{\forall x\, \forall y\, (x=y \to y=x)}\ \forall\text{Intro}}{}
$$

This proof shows that in an application of =Elim one does not have to replace all the occurrences of *a* with *b* in the step from the first to the second line. This step is licensed by the rule =Elim, taking ϕ to be the formula $x=a$. □

EXAMPLE 8.6. $\vdash \forall x\, \forall y\, \forall z\, (x=y \land y=z \to x=z)$

Proof.

$$
\dfrac{\dfrac{\dfrac{\dfrac{\dfrac{\dfrac{[a=b \land b=c]}{a=b}\ {\land}\text{Elim1} \qquad \dfrac{[a=b \land b=c]}{b=c}\ {\land}\text{Elim2}}{a=c}\ {=}\text{Elim}}{a=b \land b=c \to a=c}\ {\to}\text{Intro}}{\forall z\, (a=b \land b=z \to a=z)}\ \forall\text{Intro}}{\forall y\, \forall z\, (a=y \land y=z \to a=z)}\ \forall\text{Intro}}{\forall x\, \forall y\, \forall z\, (x=y \land y=z \to x=z)}\ \forall\text{Intro}
$$

□

This proof system, like those of propositional and predicate logic, is adequate:

THEOREM 8.7 (ADEQUACY). *Assume that ϕ and all elements of Γ are $\mathcal{L}_=$-sentences. Then $\Gamma \vdash \phi$ if and only if $\Gamma \vDash \phi$.*

As in the cases of propositional and predicate logic, I will not prove the Adequacy Theorem here.

8.5 USES OF IDENTITY

The word 'is' can play various roles. It can be used to express predication, as in 'Snow is white' or 'Jane is a classicist'. In these cases 'is' forms part of the predicate. The phrase 'is a classicist' is formalized as a unary predicate letter as it does not refer to a specific classicist.

In other cases 'is' is used to express identity as in 'Ratzinger is Benedict XVI' or 'St Mary College of Winchester is New College'. In these cases, 'is' combines two designators and expresses (numerical) identity. Thus, 'St Mary College of Winchester is New College' is formalized as $a = b$ with the obvious dictionary:

> a: St Mary College of Winchester
> b: New College

The identity symbol is useful not only for formalizing overt identity statements, as in the above examples. One can also use the identity symbol to express that there is a certain number of objects of some kind. Assume that the predicate letter Px has the following entry in the dictionary:

> P: ... is a Wagner opera

Then the claim that there is at least one Wagner opera can be expressed by existential quantification as $\exists x\, Px$. If one wants to express that there are at least two Wagner operas, however, the sentences $\exists x\, \exists y\, (Px \land Py)$ or $\exists x\, Px \land \exists y\, Py$ do not suffice, because these two sentences say merely that something is a Wagner opera and something is a Wagner opera; it does *not* say that something is a Wagner opera and something *else* is a Wagner opera. But the latter can be expressed using =:

$$\exists x\, \exists y\, (Px \land Py \land \neg x = y) \tag{8.2}$$

This sentence of $\mathcal{L}_=$ says that there are at least two Wagner operas. Of course the trick also works with three:

$$\exists x\, \exists y\, \exists z\, (Px \land Py \land Pz \land \neg x = y \land \neg x = z \land \neg y = z)$$

This sentence says that there are at least three Wagner operas.

By using identity one can also express that there is at most one Wagner opera by saying that, if x and y are Wagner operas, then x and y are identical:

$$\forall x\, \forall y\, (Px \land Py \to x = y) \tag{8.3}$$

Again this also works for 'at most two', 'at most three', and so on. 'There are at most two Wagner operas' can be formalized as

$$\forall x\, \forall y\, \forall z\, (Px \land Py \land Pz \to x = y \lor y = z \lor x = z). \tag{8.4}$$

'There is exactly one Wagner opera' can now be rephrased as 'There is at least one Wagner opera and there is at most one Wagner opera', and I have already shown how to express the two parts of that claim: $\exists x\, Px$ says that there is at least one such opera, and the second part, beginning with 'at most', has (8.3) as its formalization. So 'There is exactly one Wagner opera' can be formalized by the following $\mathcal{L}_=$-sentence:

$$\exists x\, Px \land \forall x\, \forall y\, (Px \land Py \to x = y) \tag{8.5}$$

This can also be expressed by the following logically equivalent formula:

$$\exists x\, (Px \land \forall y\, (Py \to x = y)) \tag{8.6}$$

This sentence says that there is a Wagner opera and it is the only one, that is, any Wagner opera is identical with it. A still more concise version is the sentence $\exists x\, \forall y (Py \leftrightarrow x = y)$.[1]

Similarly, one can express in $\mathcal{L}_=$ that there are exactly two Wagner operas by combining (8.2) with (8.4):

$$\exists x\, \exists y\, (Px \land Py \land \neg x = y) \land \forall x\, \forall y\, \forall z\, (Px \land Py \land Pz \to x = y \lor y = z \lor x = z)$$

By this method one can express, in the language $\mathcal{L}_=$, that there are exactly 13 Wagner operas, although this $\mathcal{L}_=$-sentence will be painfully

---

[1] The equivalence to (8.6) follows from Exercise 8.5.

long. One might think that the claim that there are 13 Wagner operas involves also a claim about a mathematical object, namely the number 13. However, the claim can be formalized without using a predicate letter or constant for numbers. Therefore, one can dispense with numbers when claiming, for instance, that there are exactly 13 Wagner operas. Some philosophers have tried to dispense with numbers and other mathematical objects completely, and the examples of this section show that identity can be used to express certain claims without reference to numbers, even if these claims seem to be about numbers at first glance.

With these tricks at one's disposal one can tackle a problem with the formalization of designators such as 'the king of France', 'Claudia's garden', 'the tallest tutor of New College who can speak Latin but does not own a car', or 'the car owned by Tim'. Designators of this kind are called 'definite descriptions'. Definite descriptions cannot be adequately formalized as constants. The following argument is logically valid:

(T) The car owned by Tim is red. Therefore there is a red car.

Formalizing the definite description by a constant yields Pa for the premiss and $\exists x\,(Px \land Qx)$ for the conclusion, with the obvious dictionary:

a: the car owned by Tim
P: ... is red
Q: ... is a car

Clearly, the argument in $\mathcal{L}_2$ corresponding to the English argument (T) is not valid, that is, $Pa \nvDash \exists x\,(Px \land Qx)$.[2] By formalizing a definite description as a constant one loses all the information contained in the definite description. As the examples above show, a definite description can contain a lot of information, and condensing 'the tallest tutor of New College who can speak Latin but does not own a car' into a single constant is bound to be inadequate.

If Tim did not own a car at all, the premiss 'The car owned by Tim is red' would not be true; if Tim owned two or more cars the premiss

---

2 See Exercise 5.2(i).

would also be not true, as there would not be any car that is *the* car owned by Tim. The premiss implies that Tim owns exactly one car. In fact, the premiss can be rephrased as follows:[3]

Tim owns exactly one car and it is red.

From the above it is clear how to express the claim that there is exactly one car owned by Tim. So the sentence can be rephrased in the following way:

There is a car owned by Tim, and it's his only car (that is, every car Tim owns is identical with it), and it is red.

Following the pattern of (8.6), the premiss of (T) is formalized as follows:

$$\exists x \left((Qx \land Rbx) \land \forall y \left(Qy \land Rby \rightarrow x=y \right) \land Px \right) \qquad (8.7)$$

The entries for b and R in dictionary are as follows:

b: Tim
R: … owns …

When the definite description 'the car owned by Tim' was formalized as a constant, the validity of (T) could not be captured by the validity of its formalization. This was the motive for seeking a more refined analysis of the definite description. I still have to show that the new, more detailed analysis actually allows me to show the validity of (T) by establishing the validity of its translation. The premiss now is formalized as (8.7) and the conclusion as before by $\exists x \left(Px \land Qx \right)$. With this formalization the argument is valid in predicate logic with identity:

EXAMPLE 8.8.

$\exists x \left((Qx \land Rbx) \land \forall y \left(Qy \land Rby \rightarrow x=y \right) \land Px \right) \vdash \exists x \left(Px \land Qx \right)$

The proof is on the next page.

---

3 The following is Russell's (1905) theory of definite descriptions. For a criticism of Russell's theory see Strawson (1950).

$$\cfrac{\cfrac{\cfrac{[((Qc \land Rbc) \land \forall y(Qy \land Rby \to c=y)) \land Pc]}{(Qc \land Rbc) \land \forall y(Qy \land Rby \to c=y)}}{\cfrac{Qc \land Rbc}{Qc}} \qquad \cfrac{[((Qc \land Rbc) \land \forall y(Qy \land Rby \to c=y)) \land Pc]}{Pc}}{\cfrac{Pc \land Qc}{\exists x(Px \land Qx)} \text{∃Intro}}$$

$$\cfrac{\exists x((Qx \lor Rbx) \land \forall y(Qy \land Rby \to x=y) \land Px) \qquad \cdots}{\exists x(Px \land Qx)} \text{∃Elim}$$

Table 8.1: Proof of Example 8.8

In some cases it may not be so easy to see that a sentence contains a definite description. Especially identity statements involving definite descriptions may be confusing. Consider the following two sentences:

(i) Jane is a classicist.
(ii) Jane is the classicist.

In the first sentence 'is' expresses predication. Sentence (ii), however, is an identity statement: 'Jane' is a proper name, while 'the classicist' is a definite description. If '… is a classicist' is translated as Q_1 and 'Jane' as c_1, sentence (i) becomes Q_1c_1, while (ii) becomes the following formula, when formalized in the style of 8.7:

$$\exists x \, (Q_1x \wedge \forall y \, (Q_1y \rightarrow y=x) \wedge c_1=x)$$

This sentence is logically equivalent to

$$Q_1c_1 \wedge \forall y (Q_1y \rightarrow y=c_1),$$

which says that Jane and only Jane is a classicist.[4]

The following example of a sentence containing a definite description is due to Russell (1905):

The king of France is bald.

By 'the king of France' I mean 'the present king of France'. Thus, this definite description does not refer to any object because France is a republic, not a monarchy. Applying the strategy above, one can rephrase this sentence as follows:

There is exactly one king of France, and he is bald.

This English sentence can be formalized as a sentence expressing that there is a king of France, he is the only king of France, and he is bald:

$$\exists x \, (Rxc \wedge \forall y \, (Ryc \rightarrow y=x) \wedge Px)$$

---

4 Someone might retort that (i) can be analysed as an identity statement as well, because it says that Jane is identical with some classicist. See Exercise 8.3 for this analysis.

R: … is a king of …
c: France
P: … is bald

Since France is a republic, the sentence 'The king of France is bald' is false. However, the sentence

$$\text{The king of France is not bald} \qquad (8.8)$$

is also false under at least one reading: it seems to say that there is exactly one king of France and that he is not bald, which is also not true since there is no king of France.

The following sentence, in contrast, is true:

It is not the case (for whatever reason) that the king of France is bald.
$$(8.9)$$

Here the claim that the king of France is bald is rejected: it leaves open whether there is a king of France who is not bald or whether there is no king of France at all, or, perhaps, whether there is more than one king, so that there is nothing that is *the* king of France.

Sentence (8.8) is most naturally formalized by the following sentence:

$$\exists x \, (Rxc \wedge \forall y \, (Ryc \to y = x) \wedge \neg Px) \qquad (8.10)$$

This says that there is a king of France, that he is the only king of France, and that he is not bald. So only the baldness is denied, not that there is exactly one king of France.

Whereas in 8.10 the negation symbol directly precedes Px, in the formalization of (8.9) it is at the beginning:

$$\neg \exists x \, (Rxc \wedge \forall y \, (Ryc \to y = x) \wedge Px) \qquad (8.11)$$

This expresses that it is not the case (for whatever reason) that there is a king of France, who is the only one, and who is bald.

If these formalizations are correct, then (8.8) and (8.9) have different meanings. But especially the formalization of (8.8) is not uncontroversial, and there may be another reading of (8.8) that results in a different formalization. The following claim is a valid argument only if (8.8) is understood as expressing the same as (8.9):

The king of France is not bald; for there is no king of France.

The first sentence is the conclusion, the second sentence is the premiss of the argument. It can be formalized as a valid argument in $\mathcal{L}_=$ only if (8.8) is formalized like (8.9) as (8.11). Thus, depending on the reading, there are two formalizations of (8.8) in $\mathcal{L}_=$ that are not logically equivalent, namely (8.10) and (8.11). If an English sentence has two non-equivalent formalizations, it is ambiguous. By comparing (8.10) and (8.11), one can see that this is a case of a scope ambiguity again. In formalization (8.10) the occurrence of $\neg$ has a 'narrow' scope; its scope is only $\neg Px$. In formalization (8.11) the negation symbol has a 'wide' scope: its scope is the entire sentence. Which formalization is better has to be decided from case to case, depending on the context.

The analysis of definite descriptions just sketched allows one to treat the expression 'the king of France' as an expression that does not refer to an object in any case. This is an advantage, compared to a formalization of 'the king of France' as a constant: a constant has exactly one object as its semantic value in any given $\mathcal{L}_2$-structure; a constant refers to an object in any $\mathcal{L}_2$-structure. If a constant is used, the following argument comes out as valid in $\mathcal{L}_=$:

It is not the case that the king of France is bald. Therefore something is not bald.

Let the constant a stand for 'the king of France'. Then $\neg Pa \vdash \exists x \, \neg Px$ can be established by a single application of the rule $\exists$Intro. However, the English argument clearly is not valid. The formalization is valid, while the English argument is not, because the semantics of constants in $\mathcal{L}_2$ and of definite descriptions in English are different: in $\mathcal{L}_2$ constants always refer to some object, while in English definite descriptions such as 'the king of France' may fail to refer to an object.

If the premiss 'It is not the case that the king of France is bald' is formalized as (8.11)

$$\neg \exists x \, (Rxc \wedge \forall y \, (Ryc \to y = x) \wedge Px),$$

in accordance with the above proposed analysis of definite descriptions, then its formalization correctly comes out as not valid. This example shows that, at least in some cases, the proposed theory of definite descriptions can be used to handle English designators that do not denote anything.

So far I have formalized proper names as constants. In the light of what has just been said, one may doubt the universal adequacy of this formalization of proper names: a proper name such as 'Pegasus' does not seem to refer to an object (existing now or in the past). One proposal for dealing with this problem is to formalize proper names in the same way as definite descriptions. But doing so requires a predicate that singles out Pegasus, such that Pegasus, if he existed, would be the one and only object satisfying this predicate. Logicians have also played with alternative semantics, where constants may fail to refer to an object. All of these proposals are beyond the scope of this text.

This discussion of definite descriptions shows that the identity symbol of $\mathcal{L}_=$ is used for more than just formalizing overt identity statements in English. Many more sentences and arguments can be analysed using identity. So formalizations in $\mathcal{L}_=$ capture more details than formalizations in $\mathcal{L}_2$. Consequently, there are English arguments that can be shown to be valid in predicate logic with identity but not in predicate logic without identity. The argument (T) above is such an argument.

Of course, strictly speaking I still have to explain what I mean by validity of an argument in predicate logic with identity, but the explanation should be obvious:

Validity of English arguments (and logical truth etc.) in predicate logic with identity is defined analogously to validity of arguments in propositional and predicate logic in Definitions 3.6, 7.8, 3.5, and 7.7.

8.6 IDENTITY AS A LOGICAL CONSTANT

Prima facie identity seems to be merely another binary predicate in English. In the semantics of $\mathcal{L}_=$, however, the identity symbol is always interpreted as numerical identity, while other binary predicate letters can be interpreted as arbitrary binary relations. Why does identity receive this special treatment? Why is there not a predicate logic with special treatment for other binary predicates such as 'is smaller than' or 'loves'? One could come up with a special symbol for any of those binary predicates and invent a semantics in which they are always interpreted in the same way. Why is identity singled out as a logical predicate, while others are not? I shall illustrate the different treatment of identity and other relations by considering two examples.

In predicate logic with identity the following argument is valid:

> The morning star is the evening star. The morning star is a planet. Hence the evening star is a planet.

In $\mathcal{L}_=$ the premisses can be formalized as $a = b$ and Pa and the conclusion as Pb. The claim $a = b, Pa \vDash Pb$ can easily be established by a proof in Natural Deduction.

In predicate logic without identity, the best possible formalization of the premisses is Rab, Pa and of the conclusion Pb, with an entry in the dictionary for Rxy as '… is identical with …'. But, by specifying an $\mathcal{L}_2$-structure in which Rab and Pa are true, and Pb is not, $Rab, Pa \vDash Pb$ can easily be refuted. Thus, the above argument is valid in predicate logic with identity but not in predicate logic without identity. The reason is that in $\mathcal{L}_=$ the interpretation of = is fixed, while in $\mathcal{L}_2$ the binary predicate letter R may be interpreted as any arbitrary binary relation.

The argument can be compared with the following argument:

> The evening star is smaller than Uranus. Uranus is smaller than Saturn. Therefore the evening star is smaller than Saturn.

This argument is not valid in predicate logic without identity or in predicate logic with identity. If the interpretation of 'smaller than' were fixed in the way the interpretation of identity is fixed in $\mathcal{L}_=$, that is, if the predicate letter for '... is smaller than ...' were always interpreted as the smaller-than relation, the argument would come out as valid. Generally, fixing the interpretation of further predicates, such as 'is smaller than', will make more arguments valid and more sentences logically true, but it is doubtful whether such notions of validity still capture logical validity and logical truth.

In Characterization 1.9 of valid arguments in Section 1.5 I stipulated that an argument is valid if and only if there is no interpretation under which the premises are all true and the conclusion is false. In interpretations, only the vocabulary that is non-logical can be reinterpreted. Logical vocabulary has been characterized as not subject-specific. The predicate expression 'is smaller than' is arguably subject-specific because it can only be sensibly applied to objects with spatial extension (and perhaps to numbers); at least it is not so clear whether it can be applied to objects such as thoughts, properties, laws, or functions. Identity, in contrast, is not specific to any subject. Thus, it cannot be reinterpreted. Logicians say that identity is a logical constant. This way of distinguishing logical from non-logical vocabulary is far from being clear and precise, and the distinction and the possibility of such a distinction are controversial issues in the philosophy of logic.

Of course there could still be expressions in English that, while not contained as logical symbols in $\mathcal{L}_=$, are logical expressions nevertheless. In fact, many logicians believe that the language $\mathcal{L}_=$ ought to be extended so as to include additional logical symbols expressing, for instance, 'it is necessary that ...'. Consequently, they think that there are valid arguments in English that are not valid in predicate logic with identity. Other philosophers think that any valid argument of English can be formalized as a valid argument in $\mathcal{L}_=$, so long as certain formalization tricks are allowed. These controversies are not only crucial for the philosophy of logic and language, they also impinge on ontology and other core disciplines of philosophy.

At any rate, $\mathcal{L}_2$ and $\mathcal{L}_=$ are very powerful languages. Many logicians, mathematicians, and philosophers believe that $\mathcal{L}_=$ is sufficient for formalizing very comprehensive parts, if not all, of mathematical and scientific discourse. If the language of mathematics and science can indeed be handled in the language of predicate logic with identity, there is hope that it can even capture large parts of philosophy.

Appendix: Natural Deduction Rules

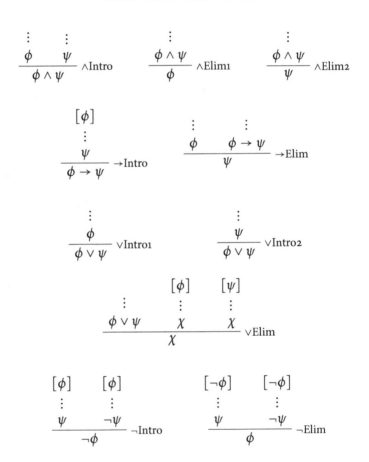

$$\frac{\phi \qquad \psi}{\phi \wedge \psi} \; \wedge\text{Intro} \qquad \frac{\phi \wedge \psi}{\phi} \; \wedge\text{Elim1} \qquad \frac{\phi \wedge \psi}{\psi} \; \wedge\text{Elim2}$$

$$\frac{\psi}{\phi \to \psi} \; \to\text{Intro} \qquad \frac{\phi \qquad \phi \to \psi}{\psi} \; \to\text{Elim}$$

$$\frac{\phi}{\phi \vee \psi} \; \vee\text{Intro1} \qquad \frac{\psi}{\phi \vee \psi} \; \vee\text{Intro2}$$

$$\frac{\phi \vee \psi \qquad \chi \qquad \chi}{\chi} \; \vee\text{Elim}$$

$$\frac{\psi \qquad \neg\psi}{\neg\phi} \; \neg\text{Intro} \qquad \frac{\psi \qquad \neg\psi}{\phi} \; \neg\text{Elim}$$

$$\frac{\begin{array}{cc} [\phi] & [\psi] \\ \vdots & \vdots \\ \psi & \phi \end{array}}{\phi \leftrightarrow \psi} \leftrightarrow \text{Intro}$$

$$\frac{\begin{array}{cc} \vdots & \vdots \\ \phi \leftrightarrow \psi & \phi \end{array}}{\psi} \leftrightarrow \text{Elim1} \qquad \frac{\begin{array}{cc} \vdots & \vdots \\ \phi \leftrightarrow \psi & \psi \end{array}}{\phi} \leftrightarrow \text{Elim2}$$

PREDICATE LOGIC

$$\forall \text{Intro} \ \frac{\begin{array}{c} \vdots \\ \phi[t/v] \end{array}}{\forall v \phi}$$

provided the constant t does not occur in ϕ or in any undischarged assumption in the proof of $\phi[t/v]$.

$$\frac{\begin{array}{c} \vdots \\ \forall v \phi \end{array}}{\phi[t/v]} \ \forall \text{Elim} \qquad \frac{\phi[t/v]}{\exists v \phi} \ \exists \text{Intro}$$

$$\exists \text{Elim} \ \frac{\begin{array}{cc} & [\phi[t/v]] \\ \vdots & \vdots \\ \exists v \phi & \psi \end{array}}{\psi}$$

provided the constant t does not occur in $\exists v \phi$, or in ψ, or in any undischarged assumption other than $\phi[t/v]$ in the proof of ψ.

IDENTITY

$$\frac{[t = t]}{\vdots} =\text{Intro}$$

$$\frac{\begin{array}{cc} \vdots & \vdots \\ \phi[s/v] & s = t \end{array}}{\phi[t/v]} =\text{Elim} \qquad \frac{\begin{array}{cc} \vdots & \vdots \\ \phi[s/v] & t = s \end{array}}{\phi[t/v]} =\text{Elim}$$

Bibliography

Cappelen, Herman and Ernest LePore (2009), Quotation, *in* E. N.Zalta, ed., 'The Stanford Encyclopedia of Philosophy', fall 2009 edition, http://plato.stanford.edu/archives/fall2009/entries/quotation/

Church, Alonzo (1936), 'A note on the Entscheidungsproblem', *Journal of Symbolic Logic* 1, 40–1.

De Morgan, Augustus (1847), *Formal Logic*, Taylor & Walton, London.

Devlin, Keith (1993), *Fundamentals of Contemporary Set Theory*, 2nd edn., Springer-Verlag, New York.

Geach, Peter (1962), *Reference and Generality*, Cornell University Press, Ithaca.

Gentzen, Gerhard (1935), 'Untersuchungen über das natürliche Schließen', *Mathematische Zeitschrift* 39, 176–210, 405–565, English translation in *The Collected Papers of Gerhard Gentzen*, M.E. Szabo (ed.), North Holland, 1969, 68–131.

Halmos, Paul R. (1960), *Naive Set Theory*, D. Van Nostrand Company, Princeton. Reprinted, Springer-Verlag, New York, NY, 1974.

Jaśkowski, Stanisław (1934), 'On the rules of supposition in formal logic', *Studia Logica* 1, 5–32, reprinted in *Polish Logic 1920-1939*, S. McCall (ed.), Oxford University Press, 1967, 232–258.

Lewis, David (1973), *Counterfactuals*, Harvard University Press, Cambridge MA, reissued in 2001 by Blackwell, London.

Morris, Charles (1938), *Foundations of the Theory of Signs*, University of Chicago Press, Chicago.

Moschovakis, Yiannis (1994), *Notes on Set Theory*, undergraduate texts in mathematics, 2nd edn., Springer, New York.

Quine, Willard Van Orman (1940), *Mathematical Logic*, Norton, New York, new edition 1951 by Harvard University Press (Cambridge MA).

Quine, Willard Van Orman (1951), 'Two dogmas of empiricism', *The Philosophical Review* 60, 20–43, reprinted in *From a Logical Point of View*, Harvard University Press 1953.

Russell, Bertrand (1905), 'On denoting', *Mind* 14, 479–93.

Sainsbury, Mark (2001), *Logical Forms*, 2nd edn., Blackwell, Oxford.

Strawson, Peter F. (1950), 'On referring', *Mind* 59, 320–44.

Tarski, Alfred (1936), 'Der Wahrheitsbegriff in den formalisierten Sprachen', *Studia Philosophica Commentarii Societatis Philosophicae Polonorum* 1, 261–404, English translation in his *Logic, Semantics, Metamathematics*, Clarendon Press 1956, 152–278.

Tennant, Neil (1990), *Natural Logic*, 2nd edn., Edinburgh University Press, Edinburgh.

Troelstra, Anne S. and Helmut Schwichtenberg (1996), *Basic Proof Theory*, number 43 Cambridge Tracts in Theoretical Computer Science, Cambridge University Press, Cambridge.

Index

Lightning Source UK Ltd.
Milton Keynes UK
UKHW021333290721
387958UK00001B/3

9 780199 587841